Literary Echoes of Gita

Reflections on interpretations by Sant Dnyaneshwar and Lokmanya Tilak

(Foreword by Dr Ravin Thatte, Plastic Surgeon, Philosopher, Environmentalist and Author of "The Geeta Revisited")

by

Sameer Godbole

समीर गोडबोले

First Edition
2024

INDIA • SINGAPORE • MALAYSIA

ISBN
Hardcase 979-8-89610-333-2
Paperback 979-8-89588-266-5

To Shakuntala, my 'Aaji' (Grandmother)

Wish you were around

ॐ नमो जी आद्या । वेद प्रतिपाद्या ।
जय जय स्वसंवेद्या । आत्मरूपा ॥ १ ॥

(Om! I bow to that primeval being, described in the Vedas!
Victory to the Self, that only the Self knows, the pristine nature of Self!)

Table of Contents

Foreword

By Dr. Ravin Thatte

Is it possible or even worthwhile to write a book on two texts based on the Geeta one of which was narrated and the other formally written almost six hundred years apart in history? That question was uppermost in my mind when I received Mr. Sameer Godbole's the then untitled manuscript on that subject. I therefore contemplated for a few days on those three texts before penning this piece.

Dnyaneshwari was narrated by Dnyaneshwar in the year 1291 CE and Tilak's Geeta Rahasya was first published in 1915 though it was written a couple of years earlier. But the common link between the two was the Geeta by far the most well-known among India's philosophical literature on which these two texts were based. But perhaps here the commonality ends somewhat because Dnyaneshwari was narrated when the Indic civilization was entering what was to be a prolonged low ebb which was to last for almost a 500-year period. In contrast, Tilak was writing at a time when the ebb had started turning into a tide. No one will ever perhaps know why Dnyaneshwar narrated in one go 9,000 exquisite verses in Prakrut/Marathi on the 700 verses of the Geeta compiled in the classical Sanskrit language because there is almost no documented historical evidence about his life and times. But traditional stories of the ostracization of Dnyaneshwar's family by the then priestly class though Dnyaneshwar was himself a Brahmin, are now a part of the folklore of the Marathi people. It was when the ostracization was lifted because the priestly class was convinced of its folly because of Dnyaneshwar's extraordinary defense of his family's circumstances by quoting extensively from the sacred texts in Sanskrit that he probably decided that the then extant sacred knowledge in Sanskrit was being misinterpreted and needed to be spread in the common people in their own language and he chose the Geeta for this purpose. It was this audacious act which made a well-known poet of recent times to call him the "the first rebel". And this act of rendering the sacred texts in a provincial language was perhaps the first such act in the history of India. And what is more, it was more than 200 years before William Tyndel accused of heresy and impiety was burnt alive at the stake for translating the New Testament from the Greek into English for the common people.

Said Dnyaneshwar about the Geeta

> *Each time I read the Geeta*
> *she appears new*
> *and with her every reading*
> *she renews me anew*

The reasons for this verse are not far to seek. As I wrote in my English translation of the Dnyaneshwari. "Geeta is not entirely new in content nor was she suddenly revealed but grew by accretion over several centuries to reflect the collective philosophical wisdom of the ages in which she grew in content over a thousand years. It has also been speculated that the theistic content in the Geeta was a necessary unavoidable later addition to the original text to accommodate the natural inclination in most of us towards the idea of God. If the Mahabharat the longest epic narrated in human history and of which Geeta is a part was a rich tapestry of the recurrent human drama over the ages the Geeta in a way is a similar rich tapestry of philosophical currents, then extant. She the Geeta devotes in equal measure of her text to devotion, action, and contemplation for realization of the ultimate truth which is the subject of the Geeta without deviating from its theistic underpinning. The one stream of philosophy that the Geeta perhaps does not do justice to is the Patanjali yogic school about which there are a mere five or six verses in the sixth chapter of the Geeta. Dnyaneshwar fills this void with aplomb by frequently mentioning the methods of that school to help the protagonist in the Geeta to achieve peace. In my mind the canard that the Yogic school is all mysticism is utterly false. It is a system which came to be revealed intuitively and deals magnificently with the autonomic nervous system the very essence of our existence. And because respiration is both voluntary and involuntary it is considered as the lynchpin through which the yogic methods are practiced. Barring that addition Dnyaneshwar in his Dnyaneshwari follows the Geeta in her letter and spirit in all her dimensions including her theistic content. The lone mission of Dnyaneshwar was to make available knowledge both of the material and spiritual world to the common people in their own language. He may have been a rebel but was not a revolutionary leader leading some mission. But his exquisite poetic work has survived in the minds of the Marathi people through the initial age of the ebb and now in the age of the incoming tide without an iota of marketing. In the words of the great Indian poet Bhavbhooti, Dnyaneshwar perhaps said to himself:

I am not in the business of reform or treason
It is just that my heart gave me the reason
For what I have written
He did not have a complaint against the then hierarchy but only compassion
for his people

Tilak who wrote the Geeta Rahasya while in a British jail during India's freedom movement was multifaceted and extraordinarily versatile to say the least. He was an editor of two dailies, both critical of the British rule. He was also a mathematician an astronomer and the creator of an Indian almanac. He established educational institutions and researched the Aryan settlements in the northwest of India based on references from ancient Sanskrit literature on which he had a profound grip. He was also a trade unionist while being in the forefront of India's freedom struggle and a frequent litigator for public causes and a social reformer. He saw in the Geeta which was revered by Indians a means to galvanize the Indian population into action as opposed to a life of renunciation of which there are albeit some shades in the Geeta and which had become a way of life in the preceding moribund 500 years. With the greatest regard to him it is obvious for a student of his work the Geeta Rahasya that he in that work written in Sanskritised Marathi with copious references from both the western and Indian philosophy that he utilized the text to stress on pragmatic action rather than devotion and contemplation. In western parlance he could be called a utilitarian philosopher. He did not refer to the Dnyanshwari while writing his magnificent tome but admitted that by all means Dnyaneshwari was a uniquely independent work on the Geeta.

Lastly his Geeta Rahasya was mainly read by the middle and upper classes who constituted the opinion makers in the struggle against the British but not by the subalterns. The readers of Dnyaneshwari belonged to all classes.

After these thoughts in my mind had crystalized, I read Mr. Godbole's manuscript in some detail. His English is excellent but easy to read a rare example in these days of mongrelisation of all languages. He brings to bear on his manuscript his extensive reading on various subjects and fits the matter in his text at appropriate places because his ideas are clear as to what he wants to convey and emphasize. The subject that he has chosen has not been dealt with extensively in the past certainly not in English and in this he succeeds greatly. The latter half of the book devoted to the current world view and the importance of texts such as these in shaping it are heartwarming. The text bears evidence of his scholarship as well as his painstaking attitude to detail.

The thesis about circumstances influencing creative work through the ages has been more than proved in this book. The fact that exceptional persons also influence the social and intellectual environment has been briefly touched in this book and perhaps could have been enlarged.

Mr. Godbole is an accountant by profession in a branch of a multinational company dealing in green energy, an avid biker, and interests in the dramatic arts and therefore a well-rounded successful person. Yet he is modest in his core and is willing to listen to suggestions. When I mentioned to him that his description of Dnyaneshwar's elucidation on the Geeta was unfairly loaded in favor of mysticism and devotion he listened, went back to his manuscript, and later agreed to alter the text after we had discussed the matter over a cup of tea. He is a seeker not pontifical. In the end I come back to the question I asked myself at the beginning. The answers are in the affirmative. Indeed, it is possible and worthwhile to compare texts so far apart in history and what is more the author has succeeded in this effort brilliantly.

This is Mr. Godbole's first major book and that too on a difficult subject and he has passed this test with flying colors. I wish him well in his future endeavors

– Dr. Ravin Thatte
MS, FRCS (Edin) Ad Hominem
Plastic and Reconstructive Surgeon, Philosopher,
Author, and Environmentalist

Preface

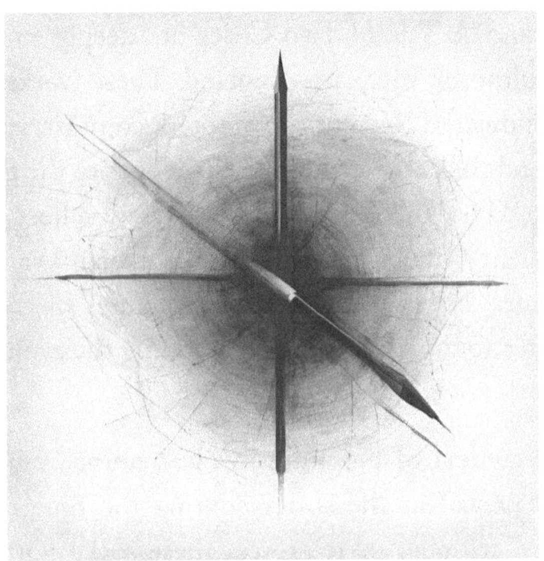

I

Every significant piece of literature is situated in a particular historical, social, and political context of its time. Literature is often a reflection of its era. The contextual elements shape the themes and narrative styles within the literary works and provide readers with insights into the socio-economic-political-moral fabric, prevailing ideologies, challenges, and transformations of a particular period. As each age leaves its indelible mark on literary expression, the resulting body of work not only reflects the unique challenges and triumphs of its time but also contributes to an evolving dialogue that continues to resonate with future generations. Understanding the contextual significance of literature enables a deeper appreciation of its relevance and impact, both in its original time and in subsequent eras.

The historical context of a literary work encompasses the events, movements, and societal changes that influence its creation. Literature often captures the essence of historical moments, preserving the collective memory of a society and offering commentary on the events that define an era. For example, Charles Dickens's novels, such as 'Oliver Twist' and 'A Tale of Two Cities' are deeply embedded in the historical backdrop of Victorian England. These works highlight the effects of the Industrial Revolution, the stark contrast between the rich and the poor, and the socio-economic challenges of the time. Similarly, Homer's epics, 'The Iliad' and 'The Odyssey' reflect the historical context of ancient Greece, particularly the Trojan War. These works mirror the values, beliefs, and societal structures of the time. These epics help form a foundation for understanding the evolution of Greek culture and mythology.

The social context of literature involves norms, values, and social dynamics that prevail in the society during the time of its creation. Literature often critiques or reinforces these social norms, addressing issues such as class, gender, race, and power dynamics. Jane Austen's novels, such as 'Pride and Prejudice' and 'Sense and Sensibility,' provide a window into the social fabric of early 19th-century England. Austen's satirical tone reveals the intricacies of social class, marriage, and the limited roles available to women. Harper Lee's 'To Kill a Mockingbird addresses the social context of the American South during the 1930s. The novel deals with issues of racism, segregation, and moral integrity, providing a poignant narrative on the social injustices and prejudices that prevailed at the time.

The political context of literature encompasses the power structures, government policies, and political ideologies that influence plots and narratives. Literature often serves as a platform for political expression, advocacy, and protest while reflecting the tensions and hopes of the political landscape. George Orwell's '1984' is a prime example of a literary work rooted deeply in its political circumstance. Written in the aftermath of World War II and during the rise of totalitarian regimes, '1984' explores themes of surveillance, propaganda, and state control. Orwell warns against the perils of unchecked political power and the erosion of personal freedom. Deeply troubled by totalitarian leaders such as Adolf Hitler and Josef Stalin, Orwell reflects the anxieties of the world grappling with totalitarianism through his novel '1984'. Salman Rushdie's 'Midnight's Children' is another work that is profoundly influenced by its political ambience. The novel spans the period of India's independence from the British rule and the subsequent dark phase of partition. Through his protagonist, Rushdie probes into the political upheavals, identity crises, and cultural transformations that accompanied the birth of a new nation. The novel's magical realism offers a multifaceted exploration of the political forces shaping modern India.

The contextual significance of literature is paramount to understanding its themes, narratives, and impact. Each important piece of literature is inextricably linked to the historical, social, and political references of its era, offering readers a lens through which to view and understand the complexities of the time. By situating literary works within their contexts, we gain not only a deeper appreciation for the artistry and insight of the authors but also a richer understanding of the human experience across different epochs. Through, the exploration of historical events, social dynamics, and political ideologies, literature becomes a repository of collective memory and cultural critique. It reflects the aspirations, struggles, and transformations of societies, providing a timeless commentary on the human condition. Whether through the depiction of historical events, the critique of social norms, or the exploration of political ideologies, literature remains a vital medium for capturing the essence of an era and fostering a deeper understanding of the world around us.

II

One of the primary goals behind this enterprise is to appreciate the fascinating transition of literature between centuries. Observing the transitions of Indian literature across different eras and decades unveils the diverse landscape of cultures, languages, and traditions that define the subcontinent. From ancient texts imbued with myth and philosophy to modern narratives reflecting the complexities of a rapidly changing society, Indian literature reflects the diverse and dynamic evolution of thought and expression over millennia. The earliest Indian literature, encapsulated in the Vedas and Upanishads, offers insights into the spiritual and philosophical foundations of Hinduism, exploring profound questions of existence, karma, and dharma. These texts, composed in Sanskrit, laid the groundwork for subsequent literary developments, influencing both religious discourse and artistic expression. The transition to the classical period witnessed the flourishing of epic poetry, most notably the Ramayana and Mahabharata, which continue to resonate as timeless narratives of heroism, duty, and moral dilemmas. These epics not only shaped literary conventions but also became cultural touchstones, inspiring generations of poets, playwrights, and storytellers across India. The medieval era marked a period of linguistic diversity and cultural synthesis, as regional languages such as Marathi, Tamil, Telugu, Kannada, and Bengali flourished under the patronage of regional kingdoms and empires. Bhakti and Sufi poets, including Dnyaneshwar, Tukaram, Kabir, Mirabai, and Tulsidas, infused their verses with devotion and mysticism, bridging the gap between religious traditions and fostering a sense of spiritual unity among diverse communities. With the arrival of European colonial powers in the 16th century, Indian literature experienced a significant transformation, as Persian and Arabic influences merged with European literary forms. The works of Mir Taqi Mir, Ghalib, and Amir Khusrau exemplify this synthesis, blending traditional poetic motifs with new themes of love, loss, and social critique. The 19th century witnessed a resurgence of Indian literature in provincial languages, spurred by the efforts of reformers and intellectuals seeking to reclaim Indigenous cultural heritage. The Bengal Renaissance, spearheaded by figures like Rabindranath Tagore and Bankim Chandra Chattopadhyay, revitalized literature with a renewed emphasis on nationalism, social reform, and humanism. The transition to the 20th century brought waves of literary innovation and experimentation, as Indian writers grappled with the challenges of modernity, independence, and social change. Writers like R.K. Narayan, Mulk Raj Anand, and Ismat Chughtai captured the complexities of postcolonial identity and the struggle for individual freedom in a rapidly evolving society. The post-independence era witnessed the emergence of a diverse array of voices from across India, reflecting regional identities, political upheavals, and socio-economic disparities. Writers such as Salman Rushdie, Arundhati Roy, and Vikram Seth gained international acclaim for their bold narratives that transcended geographical boundaries while exploring themes of globalization, migration, and cultural hybridity. Today, Indian literature continues to evolve in response to global trends, technological advancements, and shifting socio-political landscapes. Writers like Amitav Ghosh, Jhumpa Lahiri, and Aravind Adiga continue to push boundaries, blending traditional storytelling techniques with contemporary themes to capture the complexities of 21st-century India. In observing these transitions, one cannot help but marvel at the resilience and diversity of Indian literary traditions, which have endured through conquests, colonizations, and cultural exchanges. Each era brings its distinct voice and perspective, contributing to a vibrant mosaic of narratives that celebrate the richness of Indian heritage while embracing the complexities of modernity. This is not limited to Indian literature alone but is also reflected in the journey of world literature. The fascination lies not only in the literary achievements themselves but also in their ability to serve as a mirror reflecting the hopes, dreams, and struggles of a nation striving for unity in diversity.

As stated above, this book endeavours to comprehend how timeless works of literature transition through generations while retaining their contemporary relevance through multiple perspectives and interpretations that develop over time. Bhagavad Gita, the ancient Indian text is perhaps the best suited for this purpose. The book attempts a contemporary analysis and comparative study of the interpretations of one of the most revered texts in Hindu Philosophy – Bhagavad Gita, by Sant Dnyaneshwar and Lokmanya Bal Gangadhar Tilak, two luminaries in India's socio-political, spiritual, and intellectual history. Sant Dnyaneshwar's 13th-century literary work, "Dnyaneshwari", is a profoundly transcendental, partly mystical and a devotional masterpiece that emphasizes the unity of all existence and the path to self-realization through love, knowledge, and wisdom. In contrast, Lokmanya Tilak's early 20th-century work "Gita Rahasya", offers a rational and action-oriented interpretation, highlighting the importance of duty and ethical action in the quest for national independence, personal freedom, and social justice.

III

Within these paradigms of shifting socio-cultural-historical contexts accompanied by the evolution of literature, this book examines two notable interpretations of the Bhagavad Gita, 'Dnyaneshwari' by Sant Dnyaneshwar, and 'Gita Rahasya' by Lokmanya Bal Gangadhar Tilak. Both interpretations are unmistakably situated in their historical, social, and political context and therefore deliver wisdom clearly relevant to the times that they were created. A deeper understanding of the message delivered by these two towering personalities will only be achieved by developing an understanding of their contextual layers. In the end, a contemporary analysis and comparative study of these works only builds appreciation of the Bhagavad Gita's enduring potential to guide ethical and transformative actions even in contemporary times.

Acknowledgments

I would like to give a big shout-out to everyone who helped make this book possible.

First and foremost, I am deeply grateful to my father whose passion for reading has profoundly influenced my love for books and literature.

A heartfelt gratitude to Dr. Ravin Thatte for having agreed to read the manuscript and provide his valuable guidance on some of the key elements. His immense knowledge on the subject has been an inspiration as also his generous gesture to make my work more accurate and comprehensive. What more, he was gracious enough to agree to pen a foreword for a book that deals with a subject on which he himself is an authority.

Shout out to Antara Ray Chaudhary for having supported in the making of this book through her expertise in editing and publishing. Thanks to my cousins, Satish Tamhankar for his support and encouragement, and Anil Tilak whose 'follow-ups' pushed me to complete this book. A 'thank-you' to my family for always cheering me on. I should also acknowledge the AI technology that helped me create the images that you will see through the book.

Lastly, thanks to you, the readers. I hope you enjoy this journey as much as I did!

– **Sameer**

Introduction

The Bhagavad Gita, a timeless spiritual and philosophical text, has been a source of guidance and inspiration for centuries. Gita, as it is often referred to, is a 700-verse Hindu scripture that is part of the Indian epic Mahabharata. It is a sacred text of the Hindu religion and a classic of world literature, revered for its philosophical, spiritual, and practical teachings. The Gita is presented as a dialogue between Prince Arjuna and his charioteer, Lord Krishna on the battlefield of Kurukshetra. The dialogue addresses profound themes such as duty, righteousness, and the nature of reality. It is believed to have been composed between the fifth and the second centuries BCE, during a time of significant social and political changes in ancient India.

Significance of Bhagavad Gita

The epic Mahabharata, within which the Gita is situated, reflects the complexities of human relationships, governance, and moral dilemmas. In the midst of a great war, the Gita captures the essence of these struggles, providing a timeless narrative on the human condition and existence. The Bhagavad Gita offers profound philosophical insights that address the fundamental questions of existence. One of its central themes is the concept of Dharma or righteous duty. Arjuna, faced with the moral dilemma of fighting in a war against his relatives, is guided by Krishna to understand his duty as a warrior. The Gita teaches that one must perform their duties without attachment to the results, a principle known as Nishkama Karma. This philosophy encourages individuals to act ethically and responsibly, without being driven by selfish desires or fear of failure. Another significant philosophical concept in the Gita is the nature of the self. Krishna explains to Arjuna that the true self, or Atman, is eternal and beyond physical death. This understanding of the self as immortal and indestructible provides a foundation for the Gita's teachings on detachment and equanimity. The realization that the soul is untouched by worldly experiences helps individuals transcend suffering and achieve inner peace. The Gita also explores the idea of Yoga, presenting it as a disciplined path to spiritual realization. It identifies various forms of Yoga, including Karma Yoga (the yoga of action), Bhakti Yoga (the yoga of devotion), and Jnana Yoga (the yoga of knowledge). These paths cater to different temperaments and inclinations, making the Gita's teachings accessible to a wide audience. The Bhagavad Gita serves as a spiritual guide for individuals seeking a deeper understanding of their purpose and the nature of the divine. Krishna's teachings emphasize the importance of surrendering to a higher power and recognizing the divine presence in all aspects of life. This devotion to God, or Bhakti, is presented as a powerful means of achieving spiritual liberation. Krishna assures Arjuna that those who dedicate themselves to the divine with unwavering faith and devotion will attain eternal peace and unity with the divine. This message of divine grace and compassion provides solace and hope to those facing difficulties and uncertainties in life. The Gita's teachings on meditation, self-control, and inner discipline also offer practical tools for spiritual growth and self-realization. The ethical teachings of the Bhagavad Gita are particularly relevant in today's complex and often morally ambiguous world. The principle of performing one's duty without attachment to the outcomes encourages individuals to act with integrity and fairness, regardless of personal gain or loss. This ethical framework promotes a sense of responsibility and accountability, essential for maintaining social harmony and justice. The Gita also addresses the importance of compassion, non-violence, and respect for all living beings. Krishna's teachings emphasize that all actions should be guided by a sense of higher purpose and the well-being of others. This ethical perspective aligns with the principles of Ahimsa (non-violence) and promotes a compassionate and inclusive approach to life. The timeless wisdom of the Bhagavad Gita continues to resonate with people across the world, transcending cultural and religious boundaries. Its teachings offer valuable insights for addressing contemporary challenges, such as stress, anxiety, and the search for meaning in a fast-paced, materialistic world. The Gita's emphasis on mindfulness, self-discipline, and ethical conduct provides practical guidance for navigating the complexities of modern life. In the context of leadership and management, the Gita's principles of selfless action, detachment, and ethical decision-making have been widely acknowledged. Leaders and professionals can draw inspiration from the Gita's teachings to cultivate resilience, clarity, and a sense of purpose in their work. The concept of Karma Yoga, or selfless service, encourages individuals to contribute positively to society and the greater good. The Bhagavad Gita has also influenced numerous philosophers, writers, and thinkers outside the Hindu tradition. Its universal themes of duty, spirituality, and the nature of reality have inspired intellectual and spiritual discourse across cultures. Figures such as Mahatma Gandhi, Aldous Huxley[1], and Carl Jung[2] have drawn upon the Gita's wisdom in their work, highlighting its global significance. The Bhagavad Gita remains a cornerstone of spiritual and philosophical thought, offering timeless wisdom that transcends the boundaries of culture, religion, and historical context. Its teachings on duty, self-realization, and ethical action provide a comprehensive framework for navigating the complexities of life and achieving spiritual fulfilment. The Gita's relevance in contemporary times is evident in its continued influence on individuals and societies seeking guidance and inspiration. As we navigate the challenges of the modern world, the Bhagavad Gita's message of inner peace, ethical responsibility, and devotion to a higher purpose serves as a beacon of hope and wisdom. By embracing the Gita's teachings, individuals can cultivate a sense of balance, purpose, and harmony in their lives, contributing to a more just and compassionate world.

Its interpretations by different scholars and saints have added dimensions to the narrative, reflecting the diverse contexts in which they were written. Among the most influential interpretations are those by Sant Dnyaneshwar, a 13th-century saint, and Lokmanya Bal Gangadhar Tilak, a 20th-century nationalist leader. These works in my view are unsurpassed in their rich literary corpus.

---

1   Huxley emphasized the Gita's teachings on the oneness of all life, importance of selfless action and detachments. His interpretation aligns with the core principles in Gita which suggests that a common thread of truth runs through all major world religions and spiritual traditions *(Huxley, The Perennial Philosophy, 1945)*.

2   Carl Jung viewed Gita as a symbolic narrative that addresses the inner psychological conflicts and the process of individuation. He highlighted Gita's emphasis on duty, detachment, and self-knowledge as essential elements for achieving psychological wholeness. *(Carl Jung, Psychological Types, 1921)*

Sant Dnyaneshwar

Sant Dnyaneshwar, also known as Jñāneśvar or Jñanadeva, is one of the most revered saints and philosophers in Indian spiritual history. Born in the 13th century in Maharashtra, Dnyaneshwar's contributions to Indian spirituality and Marathi literature have left an indelible mark. His works, particularly the "Dnyaneshwari" (a commentary on the Bhagavad Gita) and "Amritanubhav" (The Experience of Nectar), are considered masterpieces that blend profound philosophical insights with devotional fervour.

Sant Dnyaneshwar was born in 1275 CE in the village of Apegaon near Paithan in Maharashtra. He was born into a family that faced significant social ostracism due to the unconventional path taken by his father, Vitthalpant Kulkarni, who renounced worldly life to take up sannyasa (renunciation) but again returned to being a householder and had children. This decision led to the family being excommunicated from their Brahmin community, subjecting them to severe hardships. Despite these challenges, Dnyaneshwar's early life was steeped in spiritual teachings. His father eventually returned to family life at the behest of his guru. Dnyancshwar received spiritual guidance from his elder brother Nivruttinath, a disciple of the Nath yogi Gahininath. This spiritual lineage profoundly influenced Dnyaneshwar, shaping his philosophical outlook and devotional practices. Dnyaneshwar's spiritual mission was rooted in the principles of the Bhakti movement, which emphasized personal devotion to God and sought to transcend rigid social hierarchies and ritualistic practices. However, it needs to be At the age of sixteen, Dnyaneshwar composed the "Dnyaneshwari," a Marathi commentary on the Bhagavad Gita. This work is significant not only for its spiritual and philosophical insights but also for its role in making religious and philosophical discourse accessible to the common people. By choosing to write in Marathi rather than

Sanskrit, Dnyaneshwar bridged the gap between the scholarly elite and the layperson, fostering a sense of spiritual inclusivity and unity. Dnyaneshwar's interpretation of the Gita stresses the unity of all beings and the presence of the divine in every aspect of life. His teachings advocate for a harmonious balance between worldly duties and spiritual pursuits, encouraging individuals to live a life of righteousness and inner realization. In addition to the "Dnyaneshwari," Dnyaneshwar also authored the "Amritanubhav," a philosophical treatise that explores the nature of reality, the self, and the divine. This work deep dives into the intricacies of Advaita (Monism) philosophy, presenting a vision of ultimate unity and the transcendence of dualistic distinctions. The influence of Kashmir Shaiva yoga on Dnyaneshwar is evident in his philosophical framework and spiritual practices, which emphasize the non-dualistic nature of reality and the importance of direct experience in the pursuit of self-realization. Kashmir Shaivism, with its focus on the unity of the individual self (*atman*) and the universal consciousness (*Shiva*), resonates deeply in Dnyaneshwar's teachings, particularly in his interpretations of the Bhagavad Gita. His work reflects the Shaiva belief in the inherent divinity of all beings and the transformative potential of recognizing one's true nature. For instance, Dnyaneshwar's concepts of *Shakti* and *Bhakti* echo the Kashmir Shaiva notion of divine energy and devotion, illustrating how personal surrender to the divine leads to spiritual awakening. This philosophical alignment not only enriches his text but also provides a robust framework for understanding the interplay between consciousness and existence, allowing readers to engage with profound spiritual truths that transcend time and tradition. Through poetic and metaphysical reflections, Dnyaneshwar guides the seeker towards an experiential understanding of the divine essence that pervades all existence.

Sant Dnyaneshwar's contributions to Marathi literature are monumental. He is credited with elevating Marathi to the status of a literary language, using it to convey complex spiritual and philosophical ideas with clarity and elegance. His poetic style is marked by its lyrical beauty, simplicity, and profound depth, making his works accessible to a wide audience. Dnyaneshwar's' choice to write in Marathi was revolutionary for his time, as Sanskrit was traditionally the language of scholarly and religious discourse. By democratizing spiritual knowledge and making it available in the regional language,[3] Dnyaneshwar empowered the common people to engage with and internalize spiritual teachings. His works laid the foundation for the rich tradition of Marathi literature and devotional poetry, influencing subsequent generations of saints and poets, including Namdev, Eknath, and Tukaram. Sant Dnyaneshwar's philosophical insights are rooted in the synthesis of various spiritual traditions, including Vedanta, Yoga, and Bhakti. His teachings emphasize the importance of realizing the oneness of all existence and the presence of the divine within oneself. He advocates for a balanced approach to life, where spiritual realization is not seen as separate from worldly responsibilities but rather as integrated into daily actions and relationships. One of the core themes in Dnyaneshwar's philosophy is the concept of the "jivanmukta," or the liberated soul who attains self-realization while still living in the world. According to Dnyaneshwar, such a realized being transcends the dualities of pleasure and pain, success, and failure, and remains rooted in the blissful awareness of their true nature. This state of liberation is accessible to

---

3   Christian Lee Novetzke explores the transformative impact of vernacular languages on religious practices and public discourse in premodern India in his book dedicated to this study. Novetzke's work explains how translations of sacred texts into regional languages democratized access to religious knowledge and fostered new forms of religious community and identity. His study underscores the role of language in shaping cultural and social movements, offering a nuanced understanding of India's historical and religious landscape through the lens of vernacularisation (Novetzke, "Quotidian Revolution by Vernacularisation, Religion, and the Premodern Public Sphere in India", 2017).

all, regardless of caste, gender, or social status, through sincere devotion, selfless action, and inner contemplation. Dnyaneshwar also places great emphasis on the role of the guru in guiding the seeker towards spiritual realization. In his works, he frequently extols the virtues of the guru-disciple relationship, highlighting the importance of humility, surrender, and trust in the spiritual journey. The guru, as a manifestation of divine wisdom, serves as a beacon of light, dispelling ignorance and leading the disciple towards the ultimate truth.

The legacy of Sant Dnyaneshwar extends far beyond his lifetime. His teachings laid the foundation for the continued growth of the Bhakti movement in Maharashtra, influencing subsequent saints and poets who carried forward his message of devotion, unity, and spiritual liberation. The "Dnyaneshwari" remains a central text in Marathi literature and devotional practice, revered for its spiritual depth and poetic beauty. Dnyaneshwar's emphasis on the accessibility of spiritual wisdom and the importance of personal devotion has had a lasting impact on the religious and cultural landscape of Maharashtra. His teachings continue to inspire millions, fostering a sense of spiritual unity and devotion that transcends social divisions. In contemporary times, Dnyaneshwar's message of inclusivity and compassion remains highly relevant, resonating with those seeking spiritual guidance in an increasingly complex and divided world. The annual pilgrimage of the Warkaris to the Vithoba temple in Pandharpur, which Dnyaneshwar himself undertook, continues to be a vibrant expression of the Bhakti tradition he championed. This pilgrimage, known as the Pandharpur Wari, attracts hundreds of thousands of devotees each year, reflecting the enduring appeal of Dnyaneshwar's teachings and the vitality of the spiritual movement he helped to shape. Through his profound philosophical insights and accessible poetic expressions, Dnyaneshwar democratized spiritual knowledge, making it available to all and fostering a sense of harmony, unity, and inclusivity.

Lokmanya Bal Gangadhar Tilak

Lokmanya Bal Gangadhar Tilak, born in 1856, is one of the most iconic figures in the history of India's struggle for independence. A nationalist, social reformer, and educator, Tilak's contributions to India's freedom movement and his influence on the socio-political landscape of his time were profound and far-reaching. Known for his fiery speeches and writings, he inspired millions to rise against British rule.

Bal Gangadhar Tilak was born on July 23, 1856, in Ratnagiri, Maharashtra, into a Chitpavan Brahmin family. His father, Gangadhar Tilak, was a schoolteacher and a Sanskrit scholar, which had a considerable influence on young Tilak's early education. Tilak was a brilliant student and showed an early interest in Indian history and culture. He completed his education in Pune, earning a degree in mathematics from Deccan College and later studying law at the Government Law College in Bombay (now Mumbai). His academic prowess was evident, but his heart was set on addressing the social and political issues plaguing India under British rule. After completing his education, Tilak started his career as a teacher but soon realized that education alone was not enough to bring about the change he envisioned for India. Alongside his friends, Gopal Ganesh Agarkar and Vishnushastri Chiplunkar, he founded the New English School in Pune in 1880, which aimed at providing modern education to Indian youth while instilling a sense of national pride and cultural awareness. Tilak believed that social reform was essential for the overall development of Indian society. He advocated for the education of women, the eradication of caste discrimination, and the promotion of swadeshi (self-reliance). He understood that true independence could only be achieved through the upliftment of society as a whole.

Tilak's foray into politics began in earnest with his involvement in the Indian National Congress (INC), which was founded in 1885. Initially, the Congress sought to achieve gradual reforms through dialogue with the British. However, Tilak's approach was more radical. He argued that self-rule (Swaraj) was the birthright of every Indian, a belief encapsulated in his famous declaration, "Swaraj is my birthright, and I shall have it. "Tilak's confrontational stance often brought him into conflict with the moderate leaders of the Congress, such as Gopal Krishna Gokhale. He criticized the moderate approach for being too conciliatory and ineffective in addressing the grievances of the Indian populace. His assertive methods earned him the title "Lokmanya," meaning "accepted by the people," signifying his immense popularity and the trust people placed in him.

Tilak was a prolific writer and used journalism as a powerful tool to disseminate his ideas and mobilize public opinion. He founded two newspapers, Kesari in Marathi, and Mahratta in English, through which he vigorously campaigned against British rule and highlighted issues of national importance. His writings were incisive and often provocative, leading to multiple arrests and imprisonments by the colonial authorities. One of Tilak's most significant contributions to Indian nationalism was his revival of the Ganesh Chaturthi and Shivaji Jayanti festivals. These public celebrations were transformed into platforms for political mobilization, fostering a sense of unity and national pride among Indians. Through these festivals, Tilak was able to reach a wide audience, instilling a collective consciousness and a spirit of resistance against British oppression. As a leader of the extremist faction within the Congress, Tilak's advocacy for direct action and his uncompromising stance on Swaraj set him apart from the moderates. His vision was for a self-reliant and self-governing India, free from the shackles of British exploitation. He championed the cause of Swadeshi, urging Indians to boycott British goods and promote indigenous industries. The partition of Bengal in 1905 by the British was a turning point in Indian politics, and Tilak played a crucial role in galvanizing public opposition to this divisive policy. The Swadeshi movement gained momentum, and Tilak's call for passive resistance and the boycott of British goods resonated with millions of Indians. His leadership during this period was instrumental in transforming the freedom struggle into a mass movement.

Tilak's defiance of British rule led to his arrest in 1908 on charges of sedition. He was sentenced to six years of rigorous imprisonment and transported to Mandalay in Burma (now Myanmar). During his imprisonment, Tilak wrote his seminal work, "Gita Rahasya,"[4] a commentary on the Bhagavad Gita. In this work, he explained the philosophy of Karma Yoga, emphasizing the importance of selfless action and duty, themes that mirrored his own life's mission. Tilak's interpretation of the Bhagavad Gita was not merely academic; it was a call to action. He drew parallels between the teachings of the Gita and the need for active resistance against injustice, thereby inspiring his followers to take up the mantle of the freedom struggle with renewed vigour.

Upon his release in 1914, Tilak returned to a country that had undergone significant political changes. The First World War had created new economic and social challenges, and the freedom movement was gaining momentum. Tilak resumed his political activities with undiminished fervour, focusing on building alliances and strengthening the nationalist cause. He played a leading role in the Home Rule Movement, alongside Annie Besant, advocating for self-governance and greater political autonomy for Indians. His efforts helped to unify various factions within the Congress and laid the groundwork for the future strategies of the Indian freedom struggle. Lokmanya Tilak passed away

---

4   In Mandalay jail, Tilak faced significant hardships. The conditions were harsh, and resources were limited. Despite these challenges, Tilak undertook the task of writing his book under trying circumstances. He had very limited access to books and reference materials, and he had to rely on whatever was available to him. His writing tools were minimal, and he used a pencil to draft his manuscript. Tilak's ability to compose such an influential work under these conditions is a testament to his dedication and intellectual rigor.

on August 1, 1920, but his legacy endures. His unwavering commitment to Swaraj, his advocacy for social reforms, and his role in mobilizing public opinion against British rule have left an indelible mark on India's history. He is remembered as one of the foremost architects of Indian nationalism, whose ideas and actions paved the way for future leaders like Mahatma Gandhi and Jawaharlal Nehru.

Lokmanya Tilak's life and work represent an important chapter in the history of India's fight for independence. His vision of Swaraj, his tireless efforts to awaken national consciousness, and his dedication to social reform have inspired generations of Indians. Tilak's legacy is not only that of a freedom fighter but also that of a thinker and reformer who believed in the power of education, self-reliance, and active resistance. His contributions continue to resonate in the collective memory of a nation that he helped to shape and liberate.

Importance of a contemporary analysis and comparative study of Interpretations of Bhagavad Gita by Sant Dnyaneshwar and Lokmanya Tilak

In today's complex and rapidly changing world, analysing and comparing these interpretations is not only necessary but also profoundly enlightening. The following sections explore the reasons why such a contemporary and comparative analysis is necessary, considering historical, philosophical, social, and political dimensions.

Appreciating the transition of literature[5]

Such an analysis and comparison shall use the Bhagavad Gita as a lens to appreciate the fascinating transitions of literature between eras reflecting

---

5   References: "A history of Literary Criticism and Theory: From Plato to the Present" by M A R Habib. This book offers an overview of literary theory and criticism, shedding light on how styles and approaches in literature have changed over time.

broader cultural shifts and evolving world views. It will be worthwhile to examine how such transitions reflect changing attitudes towards society, religion, politics, and the self, highlighting how literature both shapes and is shaped by its cultural context.

Understanding Historical Context and Evolution of Thought

Sant Dnyaneshwar's commentary on the Bhagavad Gita, known as the "Dnyaneshwari" or "Bhavartha Deepika," was a revolutionary work in the context of his time. The 13th century was marked by rigid caste systems, social hierarchies, and the dominance of orthodox Brahmanical traditions. Dnyaneshwar's work aimed to democratize spiritual knowledge and promote social harmony, making the sacred teachings of the Gita accessible to all, regardless of caste or social status. Lokmanya Bal Gangadhar Tilak, a prominent figure in the Indian independence movement, wrote his interpretation of the Bhagavad Gita, titled "Gita Rahasya" (The Secret of the Gita), in the early 20th century. This period was characterized by the struggle for independence from British colonial rule. Tilak's interpretation was heavily influenced by his political ideology and his commitment to the cause of Indian self-rule (Swaraj). He viewed the Gita as a call to action and a guide for ethical and righteous conduct in the pursuit of national freedom.

Philosophical Depth and Diverse Interpretations

Dnyaneshwar's interpretation of the Bhagavad Gita is deeply transcendental and spiritual. He emphasizes the unity of all existence and the path to self-realization through devotion (bhakti) and knowledge (jnana). His poetic and allegorical style brings out the essence of divine love and the oneness of the individual soul (atman) with the Supreme (Brahman). For Dnyaneshwar, the Gita is a guide to experiencing divine unity and transcending the illusions of the material world. In contrast, Tilak's interpretation is rational, analytical, and action oriented. He focuses on karma-yoga, the path of selfless action, arguing that the Gita advocates for active engagement in the world and the performance of one's duties according to dharma (righteousness). Tilak's pragmatic approach aligns the Gita's teachings with the needs of the nationalist movement, emphasizing duty, responsibility, and ethical conduct in the face of oppression.

Relevance to Contemporary Social Issues

Dnyaneshwar's emphasis on the unity of all existence and the accessibility of spiritual knowledge to all people is particularly relevant in today's times, where issues of social inequality, discrimination, and exclusion persist. His teachings promote values of inclusivity, compassion, and universal brotherhood, challenging the divisive forces that threaten social harmony. Analysing Dnyaneshwar's interpretation can inspire contemporary efforts to foster inclusivity and social cohesion. Tilak's focus on duty and action is equally pertinent in addressing contemporary challenges. In a world facing political turmoil, environmental crises, and social injustices, the call for ethical action and civic responsibility resonates strongly. Tilak's interpretation encourages individuals to actively participate in societal transformation and to uphold ethical principles in their personal and public lives. This perspective is essential for nurturing a sense of civic duty and collective responsibility.

Bridging Spirituality and Social Activism

The comparative analysis of Dnyaneshwar's and Tilak's interpretations highlights the potential for bridging spirituality and social activism. Dnyaneshwar's transcendental approach and Tilak's pragmatic perspective are not mutually exclusive but can be seen as complementary paths that enrich our understanding of Gita's teachings. This synthesis can inspire a comprehensive approach to personal and social transformation, integrating spiritual growth with active engagement in addressing societal issues.

Addressing Contemporary Political and Ethical Dilemmas

In today's complex political landscapes, the principles espoused by Tilak in his interpretation of the Gita offer valuable insights. His emphasis on righteous conduct and ethical governance can guide political leaders and activists in navigating ethical dilemmas and making decisions that uphold justice and integrity. Tilak's call for active resistance against oppression and injustice is relevant for contemporary movements advocating for human rights and social justice. The ethical teachings of the Bhagavad Gita, as interpreted by both Dnyaneshwar and Tilak, have universal relevance. In an increasingly interconnected world, where global ethical standards are essential for addressing transnational challenges such as climate change, human rights, and economic inequality, Gita's emphasis on duty, responsibility, and ethical action can provide a moral compass. Comparative analysis of these interpretations can contribute to global discourses on ethics and governance.

Cultural and Educational Significance[6]

Analysing and comparing the interpretations of the Bhagavad Gita by Dnyaneshwar and Tilak helps preserve and promote India's rich cultural and philosophical heritage. These interpretations are not only significant texts in their own right but also form an integral part of the varied tableau of Indian thought and spirituality. By studying these works, contemporary scholars and students can gain

---

6 References: "The Written World: How Literature Shapes History" by Martin Puchner. In here Puchner examines the role of key literary works from different cultures and epochs, illustrating how these texts have influenced political, social, and cultural developments.

a deeper appreciation of India's intellectual and cultural legacy. Incorporating the comparative study of Dnyaneshwar's and Tilak's interpretations into educational curricula can provide students with a nuanced understanding of philosophical and ethical concepts. It can also encourage critical thinking, cultural awareness, and the ability to engage with diverse perspectives. This educational approach can foster a generation of individuals who are not only well-versed in their cultural heritage but also equipped to address contemporary challenges with wisdom and integrity.

Fostering Dialogue and Understanding

The teachings of the Bhagavad Gita, as interpreted by Dnyaneshwar and Tilak, offer valuable perspectives for interfaith and intercultural dialogue. Dnyaneshwar's emphasis on the unity of all existence and Tilak's focus on ethical action can provide common ground for discussions on spirituality, ethics, and social justice across different religious and cultural traditions. Such dialogue can promote mutual understanding and cooperation in addressing global issues. The comparative analysis of these interpretations can also bridge generational gaps, fostering dialogue between older and younger generations. By exploring the historical, social, and political contexts in which these interpretations were written, contemporary readers can appreciate the relevance of these teachings in today's world. This understanding can inspire a sense of continuity and connection between past and present, enriching the collective consciousness.

Analysing and comparing the interpretations of the Bhagavad Gita by Sant Dnyaneshwar and Lokmanya Tilak is not merely an academic exercise but a profound exploration of the diverse dimensions of human experience and thought. In today's times, characterized by rapid social, political, and cultural changes, this comparative study offers valuable insights into addressing contemporary challenges with wisdom and integrity. Dnyaneshwar's' mystico-transcendental and inclusive approach and Tilak's rational and action-oriented perspective provide complementary pathways for personal and social transformation. Their teachings inspire a holistic understanding of spirituality and social activism, bridging the spaces of inner growth and external engagement. By studying these interpretations, contemporary readers can draw lessons for fostering inclusivity, ethical action, and global cooperation, contributing to a more just and harmonious world. In essence, the comparative analysis of Dnyaneshwar's and Tilak's interpretations of the Bhagavad Gita enriches our understanding of the text's timeless relevance and its potential to inspire positive change in today's complex and interconnected world.

Historical Context

Understanding the socio-economic, cultural, and political ambience that influenced the two literary works

The historical ambience of Dnyaneshwari – caste-based societal structure, bhakti movement, and the rise of Marathi

The 13th century, when Sant Dnyaneshwar lived and composed his influential works, was a period of significant transformation in India. It was a period marked by significant social, cultural, and religious transformations, providing the backdrop against which Sant

Dnyaneshwar emerged as a prominent figure in Maharashtra. The date of his composition Dnyaneshwari is recorded as 1290 CE. This era was marked by the consolidation of regional kingdoms, the penetration of Islamic rule into the Deccan, and a complex interplay of social, religious, and cultural dynamics.

During the 13th century, the Indian subcontinent was fragmented into various regional kingdoms, each vying for power and control. The Deccan region, where Dnyaneshwar was born and lived, was particularly influenced by the Yadava dynasty, which ruled over a sizeable portion of present-day Maharashtra from their capital at Devagiri (modern-day Daulatabad, Deogiri). Dnyaneshwar was born on the banks of river Godavari near Paithan during the reign of the Yadava king Ramadevarava. The Yadava dynasty, under rulers like King Singhana II, enjoyed a period of relative stability and prosperity, fostering a rich cultural and intellectual environment. It was during this period that Sarangadeva composed 'Sangita Ratnakara,' his famous treatise on music. Yadavas were the first major dynasty to adopt Marathi as an official language, replacing Sanskrit and Kannada. However, this period also saw the growing influence of the Delhi Sultanate in the Deccan. The incursions by the Sultanate, especially during the reign of Alauddin Khilji, introduced new administrative practices, military strategies, and cultural exchanges. These interactions, while often conflict-ridden, also led to a syncretic blending of Hindu and Islamic traditions, evident in the architecture, art, and social customs of the time. The political milieu was thus characterized by a dynamic tension between regional powers and the expanding influence of the Sultanate, creating an environment of both conflict and cultural amalgamation.

The social structure in 13th-century India was predominantly hierarchical and caste-based. Caste hierarchies were deeply entrenched in medieval Indian society, determining social status, occupation, and religious practices. Caste Systems divided people into groups based on their birth or occupation. The four varnas or classes were brahmins – considered to be the highest caste they were mostly priests or scholars who held positions of intellectual and religious authority; Kshatriyas – considered the second varna, the Kshatriyas were warriors, rulers, and governors who controlled political power and wealth; Vaishyas – these were merchants, farmers, cattle herders, artisans and agriculturists who dominated trade and economy; Shudras – considered the lowest varna, Shudras were labourers, servants, and service providers who bore the brunt of discrimination and exclusion from society. The rigid caste system dictated social interactions, occupations, and religious practices, leading to significant social stratification and discrimination. Brahmins, as the priestly class, held considerable influence over religious and educational matters, while Kshatriyas, Vaishyas, and Shudras were relegated to specific societal roles, often with limited mobility. Dnyaneshwar's family, belonging to the Brahmin caste, faced ostracism and persecution due to his father's unconventional decision to renounce his Brahminical duties and become a sannyasi (renunciant). This social boycott deeply affected Dnyaneshwar and his siblings, shaping his perspectives on social justice, equality, and spiritual inclusivity. The societal challenges of the time were manifold. The rigid caste system perpetuated inequality and injustice, leading to social tensions and conflicts. Furthermore, the growing influence of Islamic rulers introduced new social dynamics, sometimes resulting in cultural clashes but also promoting exchanges that enriched the socio-cultural fabric of the region. Bhakti saints like Dnyaneshwar challenged these rigid class-based divisions by advocating for spiritual equality and universal love. Their teachings attracted followers from all castes, creating communities of devotees (sampradayas) centred around shared spiritual ideals rather than birth-based distinctions.

This century witnessed a significant religious and spiritual activity in India. The Bhakti movement, which emphasized personal devotion to God and the rejection of ritualistic practices, was gaining momentum across the subcontinent. Influenced by earlier saints like Ramanuja, Basava, and Ramananda, the Bhakti movement sought to democratize spirituality, advocating direct communion with the divine irrespective of social status or caste, or gender. The movement spread across various regions of India, each contributing unique flavours to its panorama. In Maharashtra, Bhakti found expression in the provincial Marathi language through the compositions of saints like Namdev, Eknath, Tukaram, and most notably, Sant Dnyaneshwar. Saints and poets including Dnyaneshwar played a vital role in propagating the ideals of the Bhakti movement, challenging the orthodox practices, and advocating for a more inclusive and compassionate approach to spirituality. These saints composed devotional poetry and hymns (abhangas) that resonated deeply with the masses, promoting love, humility, and devotion as paths to spiritual realization. In Maharashtra, the Varkari tradition, a devotional movement dedicated to the worship of Vithoba (a form of Krishna), was gaining prominence. This tradition emphasized community worship, singing of abhangas (devotional songs), and pilgrimage to the Vithoba temple in Pandharpur. Dnyaneshwar, along with his siblings, became a key figure in the Varkari tradition, contributing significantly to its growth and popularity. This philosophical framework provided a profound intellectual basis for Bhakti saints like Dnyaneshwar, who sought to reconcile the essence of the ancient scriptures with the everyday experiences of common people. Dnyaneshwar's seminal work, the "Dnyaneshwari," a Marathi commentary on the Bhagavad Gita, reflects the inclusive and egalitarian spirit of the Bhakti movement. By writing in Marathi, the regional language, instead of Sanskrit, he made spiritual knowledge accessible to the common people, bridging the gap between the elite and the masses. His emphasis on devotion (bhakti), selfless action (karma), and knowledge (jnana) as paths to spiritual liberation resonated deeply with the populace, fostering a sense of unity and spiritual awakening.

The economic conditions in the 13th century Deccan were shaped by agriculture, trade, and crafts. The fertile plains of the region supported a thriving agrarian economy, with crops like rice, wheat, and millet being the staples. The Yadav rulers implemented various irrigation projects and land revenue systems to support agriculture, contributing to economic stability and growth. Trade and commerce also played a decisive role in the economy, with the Deccan region acting as a vital link between North and South India. The region's strategic location facilitated the movement of goods, people, and ideas, promoting economic and cultural exchanges. Artisans and craftsmen enjoyed patronage from the ruling elite, leading to the flourishing of arts, crafts, and architecture. However, the economic prosperity was not evenly distributed. The caste-based social structure often dictated economic opportunities, with lower castes having limited access to resources and opportunities for upward mobility. This economic disparity further exacerbated social tensions and conflicts.

The 13th century was a period of vibrant cultural and intellectual activity in the Deccan. The patronage of the Yadava rulers supported the growth of literature, music, art, and architecture. Sanskrit and Marathi literature flourished, with scholars and poets producing works of enduring significance. Dnyaneshwar's contributions to Marathi literature were monumental. His "Dnyaneshwari" and "Amritanubhav" (The Experience of Nectar) are masterpieces of spiritual and philosophical literature. These works not only enriched Marathi literature but also served as vehicles for propagating the ideals of the Bhakti movement. Dnyaneshwar's poetic style, marked by its lyrical beauty, simplicity, and depth, made profound philosophical concepts accessible to the common people. The cultural life of the region was also marked by the celebration of festivals, music, dance, and theatrical performances. The Bhakti movement, with its emphasis on community worship and devotional singing, played a crucial role in fostering a sense of cultural unity and shared identity.

To summarize, the socio-political context of the 13th century, marked by a period of tumult marked by external invasions and conflict, social stratification, religious transformation, and cultural vibrancy, profoundly influenced Sant Dnyaneshwar's life and work. His contributions to the Bhakti movement, his challenge to social injustices, and his efforts to democratize spiritual knowledge were deeply rooted in the realities of his time. Understanding this context is essential to appreciate the enduring significance of Dnyaneshwar's teachings and their impact on Indian spirituality and culture.

The historical ambience of Gita Rahasya – an era marked by the British rule and socio-cultural renaissance

The late 19th and early 20th centuries in India were marked by profound socio-political, cultural, and economic transformations, shaped largely by British colonial rule and Indian responses to it. This period was decisive in shaping modern India's trajectory towards independence and socio-economic progress.

British colonialism in India was characterized by economic exploitation, cultural domination, and political repression. By the late 19th century, the British had established their supremacy through administrative reforms and economic policies that systematically drained India's wealth. The exploitation of Indian resources and labour fuelled discontent among Indians across all social strata, laying the foundation for nationalist sentiments and movements. British colonialism fundamentally altered Indian society. The British East India Company's expansionist policies and subsequent direct rule by the British Crown led to a systematic reorganization of Indian governance, economy, and culture. The imposition of British administrative structures, legal systems, and economic policies aimed at exploiting India's resources for the benefit of the British Empire.

The Indian response to colonial rule was multifaceted. Initially, Indian elites collaborated with the British, hoping to modernize India through reforms and participation in the colonial administration. The late 19th century witnessed the emergence of Indian nationalism as a potent force against British imperialism. Discontent grew as the economic exploitation intensified, leading to movements for political autonomy and self-rule. The Indian National Congress (INC), founded in 1885, initially advocated for reforms within the colonial framework. However, by the turn of the century, the Congress became a platform for articulating nationalist aspirations for self-governance, civil rights, and socio-economic reforms. Leaders like Dadabhai Naoroji, Gopal Krishna Gokhale, and later, Tilak himself, played crucial roles in shaping nationalist discourse within the INC. Tilak's entry into the political scene marked a shift towards militant nationalism. He criticized the moderate approach of the early Congress leaders and advocated for more assertive measures to attain self-rule (Swaraj). Tilak's fierce nationalism and advocacy for self-rule profoundly influenced many including Veer Savarkar, inspiring him to adopt a more radical approach to independence that emphasized the importance of Hindu identity and cultural pride in the struggle against colonial rule. Tilak's ideology resonated with growing discontent among Indians, particularly after the economic hardships caused by famines and British policies. In response to British economic policies and the partition of Bengal in 1905, Tilak advocated for the Swadeshi movement and boycott of British goods. He encouraged Indians to promote indigenous industries and adopt a self-sufficient economy. The movement spread across India, becoming a symbol of resistance against colonial exploitation.

India in the late 19th and early 20th century was not only witnessing political upheaval against British colonial rule but also experiencing a surge of social reform movements that aimed to address deep-rooted social injustices and bring about progressive change within Indian society. Western education and exposure to Enlightenment ideals influenced a burgeoning middle class and intellectual elite in India, sparking a desire for reform and social progress. These movements, spearheaded by visionary leaders and reformers, challenged age-old customs, advocated for gender equality, promoted education, and fought against caste discrimination. These social reform movements of the era had a lasting impact on Indian society. These social reform movements sought to address internal issues within Indian society. The Brahmo Samaj, founded by Raja Ram Mohan Roy in 1828, laid the groundwork for social and religious reform in India. It aimed to purify Hinduism by removing social evils such as sati (widow burning), child marriage, and caste discrimination. Roy's efforts led to the abolition of sati through legislative reforms in 1829, marking a significant milestone in India's social reform movements. Swami Dayananda Saraswati founded the Arya Samaj in 1875, advocating for the revival of Vedic knowledge and principles. The Arya Samaj promoted social equality, and education for all, and opposed idol worship and superstitions. It played a crucial role in promoting Vedic education, especially among the marginalized sections of society. Later movements, led by Jyotirao Phule and B.R. Ambedkar, focused on caste reform and empowerment of marginalized communities.

The late 19th and early 20th centuries also witnessed a cultural renaissance in India, often referred to as the Bengal Renaissance. This intellectual and artistic awakening was a response to colonialism and aimed to revive and reinterpret India's rich cultural heritage amidst rapid social and political changes. Encounters with Western education, literature, and philosophy also sparked a re-evaluation of India's cultural legacy among its educated elite. Intellectuals and artists sought to revive and reinterpret India's rich cultural heritage. Figures like Rabindranath

Tagore, Bankim Chandra Chattopadhyay, and Swami Vivekananda promoted a renaissance of Indian literature, art, and philosophy. They emphasized the synthesis of traditional Indian values with modern education, scientific inquiry, and Western ideas of rationalism and humanism. Bengali literature flourished during this period with luminaries such as Rabindranath Tagore, Sarat Chandra Chattopadhyay, and Michael Madhusudan Dutt. Tagore, in particular, emerged as a towering figure with his poetry, novels, and plays that explored themes of humanism, spirituality, and social reform. His work earned him the Nobel Prize in Literature in 1913, making him the first non-European to receive the honour. The Renaissance also saw efforts to rediscover and reinterpret India's ancient cultural heritage. Scholars and archaeologists like Raja Ravi Varma and James Prinsep made significant contributions to the study of Indian history, art, and archaeology, shedding light on the rich cultural legacy that predated colonial rule. The cultural renaissance in India during the late 19th and early 20th century had a profound impact on shaping national consciousness and identity. It instilled pride in India's cultural heritage, promoted social reforms, and laid the intellectual groundwork for the nationalist movement against British colonialism. The Renaissance also fostered a spirit of intellectual inquiry and creativity that continues to influence Indian literature, art and thought to this day. It challenged colonial narratives, celebrated India's cultural diversity, and laid the foundations for the country's eventual independence. At the same time, it is ironic that it took British rule to awaken in Indians a profound awareness of their true cultural identity, as the very imposition of foreign governance highlighted the richness and depth of their own heritage.

The late 19th and early 20th centuries were transformative periods in India's economic history, marked by profound changes shaped by British colonial rule, industrialization, and the emergence of nationalist economic policies. British colonial policies had a profound impact on

India's economy. British colonial rule in India was primarily driven by economic exploitation and the extraction of resources to benefit the British Empire. The economic policies imposed by the British had far-reaching consequences for India's economy, society, and industrial development. The emphasis on cash crops, heavy taxation, and discriminatory trade policies led to the impoverishment of Indian farmers and artisans. India was historically known for its thriving handicrafts and cottage industries. However, British policies such as tariffs, monopolies, and industrial subsidies favoured British manufactured goods over Indian products. This led to the decline of indigenous industries and the deindustrialization of India, exacerbating poverty, unemployment, and discontent. Despite the exploitative economic policies, the British also initiated significant infrastructural developments in India, notably the construction of railways. The railways played a dual role: facilitating the movement of raw materials and finished goods across the subcontinent, thereby integrating regional markets, but also serving British economic interests. The introduction of railways facilitated the commercialization of agriculture by providing faster and cheaper transportation of agricultural produce to distant markets. However, this also led to increased reliance on cash crops like cotton, indigo, and jute, which displaced food crops and contributed to agrarian distress during famines. While the railways contributed to the growth of some industries such as cotton textiles and coal mining, British capitalists largely controlled these industries. Indian entrepreneurs faced stiff competition from British firms, limiting indigenous industrial growth and technological advancements. The late 19th century witnessed the emergence of nationalist economic thought, which sought to challenge British economic dominance and promote indigenous industrialization and economic self-sufficiency. Leaders like Dadabhai Naoroji and Gopal Krishna Gokhale articulated the Drain Theory, highlighting how India's wealth was drained to Britain through economic exploitation. Leaders like Bal Gangadhar Tilak and Lala Lajpat Rai advocated for economic nationalism, emphasizing the need for protective tariffs, investment in infrastructure, and support for indigenous industries. Their efforts laid the foundation for economic policies that would later shape independent India's economic development agenda. The economic history of late 19th and early 20th century India under British colonial rule was characterized by exploitative economic policies, deindustrialization, and agrarian distress. Despite these challenges, the era also witnessed the emergence of nationalist economic thought and movements that laid the groundwork for India's eventual independence and economic resurgence. The legacy of this period continues to influence India's economic policies and development strategies, emphasizing self-reliance, industrial growth, and equitable distribution of resources. Understanding India's economic history during this era provides valuable insights into the enduring impact of colonialism on developing economies and the resilience of nations in reclaiming their economic sovereignty.

The historical, socio-political, and economic ambience of late 19th and early 20th century India profoundly influenced Lokmanya Tilak's literary work, "Gita Rahasya." His interpretation of the Bhagavad Gita reflected his deep engagement with the challenges and aspirations of his times: the struggle against colonial oppression, the quest for national identity, and the promotion of social and economic justice. Tilak's "Gita Rahasya" continues to be a testament to his intellectual vigour, spiritual depth, and unwavering commitment to India's independence and cultural resurgence.

Varied ambiences leading to variation in interpretations of the same sacred text – 'Bhagavad Gita'

The differences between the socio-economic, political, and cultural environments of the 13th century and the late 19th to early 20th century highlight the evolution of Indian society under changing historical contexts. Dnyaneshwar's "Dnyaneshwari" emerged in a feudal and religiously vibrant atmosphere, emphasizing spiritual devotion and social inclusivity. In contrast, Tilak's "Gita Rahasya" represented spiritual activism which was shaped by colonial oppression, industrialization, and nationalist fervour, advocating for political autonomy, economic self-sufficiency, and cultural resurgence. These works not only reflect their respective eras but also continue to resonate in the ongoing narrative of India's socio-political evolution.

Sant Dnyaneshwar's writing style in "Dnyaneshwari" is characterized by its simplicity, poetic elegance, and profound spiritual insight. Influenced by the socio-political environment of 13th-century Maharashtra, marked by the Bhakti movement and social reformist impulses, Dnyaneshwar's commentary on the Bhagavad Gita transcends mere philosophical discourse. It becomes a powerful expression of devotion, social inclusivity, and linguistic empowerment, shaping the cultural and spiritual landscape of Maharashtra and leaving a lasting legacy in Indian literature and philosophy. On the other hand, Lokmanya Tilak's writing style in "Gita Rahasya" is characterized by its blend of scholarly analysis, spiritual depth, and nationalist fervour. Influenced by the socio-political environment of colonial India, Tilak interprets the Bhagavad Gita as a spiritual and philosophical guide for individual and national liberation. His clear and accessible language ensured that his nationalist and philosophical ideas reached a wide audience, contributing significantly to India's independence movement and cultural resurgence during that era.

Bhagavad Gita Chapter 2, Verse 47 (BG 2.47)

Sanskrit

कर्मण्येवाधिकारस्ते मा फलेषु कदाचन।
मा कर्मफलहेतुर्भूर्मा ते सङ्गोऽस्त्वकर्मणि॥ ४७ ॥

Transliteration

karmaṇyevādhikāraste mā phaleṣu kadācana
mā karmaphalaheturbhūrmā te saṅgo'stvakarmaṇi || 47 ||

Translation

"You have a right to perform your prescribed duties, but you are not entitled to the fruits of your actions. Never consider yourself to be the cause of the results of your activities, nor be attached to inaction."

Interpretations

Sant Dnyaneshwar's interpretation of Bhagavad Gita Chapter 2, Verse 47 in "Dnyaneshwari" encapsulates his profound understanding of karma yoga, bhakti, and Advaita Vedanta philosophy. His interpretation encourages individuals to engage in their prescribed duties with dedication and sincerity, while simultaneously fostering a sense of detachment from personal desires and outcomes. By surrendering to the divine will and recognizing the oneness of all existence, Dnyaneshwar guides readers toward spiritual realization and inner peace. His interpretation continues to inspire seekers of truth and spiritual wisdom, offering timeless guidance on ethical conduct, devotion, and the pursuit of liberation.

Lokmanya Tilak's interpretation of Bhagavad Gita Chapter 2, Verse 47 in "Gita Rahasya" highlights his profound understanding of Karma Yoga and its application in both personal and socio-political contexts. His interpretation encourages individuals to uphold their responsibilities with dedication and integrity, without being swayed by personal desires or attachments. Moreover, Tilak's nationalist perspective infuses this verse with a call to action for the betterment of society and the nation, reflecting his commitment to India's independence struggle and cultural resurgence. Thus, BG 2.47 in "Gita Rahasya" not only serves as a spiritual guide but also as a moral compass for righteous conduct and societal upliftment.

As you read further, you will realise that Sant Dnyaneshwar's "Dnyaneshwari" and Lokmanya Tilak's "Gita Rahasya" are both monumental interpretations of the Bhagavad Gita, driven by their respective socio-historical contexts and personal motivations. They are indeed a testimony of literature that transcends eras and remains relevant to the times while exploring universal truth and fundamental ideas.

Author's Notes:

I wish to underline the value of understanding the historical context in which a particular work of literature is situated. It allows the readers to grasp the nuances embedded within the text. For example, Charles Dickens's "A Tale of Two Cities" can be better understood when considering the impact of the French Revolution. Recognizing the historical backdrop can explain the author's motivations and influences. Knowledge of historical context can bridge the gap between contemporary readers and the period in which the work was originally written. Overall, understanding the historical context enriches our comprehension and appreciation of literary works, providing layers of meaning that are essential for thorough and informed analysis.

References

Bloom H, Charles Dickens, 2006; Reynolds D.S., Walt Whitman's America: A Cultural Biography,1995; Salt E.W., The World, the Text, and the Critic, 1983

Chapter 2

Philosophical Foundations

The philosophy of Gita

जे स्वधर्में निष्कामता । अनुसरले पार्थी ।
ते कैवल्यपद तत्त्वतां । पातले जगीं ॥ १५१ ॥

(Those who attain the state of non-attachment to the fruit of their actions and perform their duty, are the ones who attain the highest form of bliss in this world – DN 3.151)

The Mahabharata, an epic narrative of ancient India, spans various themes including ethics, politics, warfare, and spirituality. The context of the Mahabharata revolves around the struggle between the Pandavas and the Kauravas, two factions of a royal family vying for control of the kingdom. At its core lies the Bhagavad Gita, structured as a dialogue between Prince Arjuna and the god Krishna, who serves as his charioteer that takes place on the battlefield of Kurukshetra. The Bhagavad Gita, often referred to simply as the Gita, is a 700-verse Hindu scripture that is part of this ancient Indian epic and is composed in Sanskrit. Set amidst the battlefield of Kurukshetra, the Gita addresses profound philosophical and ethical dilemmas faced by Arjuna, ultimately imparting spiritual wisdom and guidance. This profound text, embedded within the epic Mahabharata, is traditionally attributed to the sage Vyasa.

Vyasa, also known as Vedavyasa or Krishna Dvaipayana Vyasa, occupies a significant place in Hindu tradition as a sage of immense wisdom and literary prowess. He is credited not only with composing the Mahabharata but also with compiling and arranging the Vedas, the oldest sacred texts of Hinduism. Vyasa's birth is said to be divine in origin; he was born to the sage Parashara and the fisherwoman Satyavati. His name, Vyasa, means "compiler" or "arranger," reflecting his role in organizing the Vedas into their current form. Vyasa is believed to have lived during the Dvapara Yuga, an era preceding the current age (Kali Yuga) in Hindu cosmology. His lineage is illustrious, and he is regarded as a master of spiritual knowledge and philosophy. Apart from the Mahabharata and its philosophical jewel, the Bhagavad Gita, Vyasa is also credited with writing the Puranas, which are important mythological and historical texts in Hinduism. The Bhagavad Gita is set on the brink of the Kurukshetra War, where Arjuna, a warrior prince of the Pandavas, faces a moral crisis and seeks guidance from Krishna, his charioteer. Arjuna is torn between his duty as a warrior (*kshatriya dharma*) and his familial ties to those standing on the opposing side, including beloved relatives and revered teachers. Krishna's teachings in the Gita address Arjuna's doubts and provide profound insights into life, duty, and spiritual liberation.

Quite like Dnyaneshwar and Lokmanya Tilak, there certainly would have been a profound purpose behind Vyasa to pen the epic Mahabharata and in that, the sacred Bhagavad Gita firmly situated in the contextual base of the time it was written (believed to be fifth or fourth century BCE). Drawing from both traditional interpretations and contemporary scholarly perspectives, multiple profound objectives could be attributed to this remarkable creation by Vyasa. One of the primary objectives behind writing the Bhagavad Gita was to provide ethical guidance in the face of moral dilemmas. Arjuna, a warrior prince, faces a crisis of conscience as he prepares to engage in battle against his kin. His dilemma mirrors universal conflicts between duty (dharma) and personal attachments. The Gita addresses this by emphasizing the importance of fulfilling one's responsibilities (Swadharma) without attachment to the outcomes of actions. It teaches that ethical conduct and adherence to duty are essential for personal growth and societal harmony. The Bhagavad Gita expounds various paths (yogas) to spiritual liberation (moksha), catering to different temperaments and inclinations of individuals. These include Karma Yoga (the yoga of selfless action), Bhakti Yoga (the yoga of devotion), and Jnana Yoga (the yoga of knowledge). By integrating these paths, the Gita provides a comprehensive framework for spiritual seekers to transcend egoic attachments and realize their true nature (atman). Another objective of the Bhagavad Gita is to reconcile seemingly divergent paths of knowledge and action. Krishna's teachings unify philosophical insights with practical guidance on righteous living. The Gita bridges the gap between contemplative spirituality and active engagement in the world, emphasizing the importance of integrating spiritual wisdom into everyday life. The teachings of the Bhagavad Gita are not confined to any particular time, place, or religious tradition. Its universal appeal lies in its timeless wisdom and practical applicability to the human condition. The Gita addresses existential questions, such as the purpose of life, the nature of suffering, and the quest for self-realization, making it relevant to individuals seeking meaning and fulfilment beyond religious boundaries. Vyasa, traditionally credited as the author of the Mahabharata and the Bhagavad Gita, intended to transmit profound spiritual knowledge to future generations. The Gita serves as a spiritual manual, imparting teachings that guide individuals on their spiritual journey and encourage them to cultivate virtues such as compassion, equanimity, and self-discipline. The dialogue between Arjuna and Krishna in the Bhagavad Gita also serves to resolve Arjuna's doubts and confusion regarding his duty and the consequences of his actions. Krishna's teachings provide clarity and perspective, empowering Arjuna to make informed choices aligned with higher principles and values. To conclude on the business of establishing the probable purpose behind scripting the Gita it is imperative to view The Bhagavad Gita as a timeless scripture that addresses existential dilemmas, ethical quandaries, and the quest for spiritual enlightenment. Its objectives encompass ethical guidance, pathways to spiritual liberation, unity of knowledge, universal relevance, transmission of spiritual wisdom, and resolution of doubt. Through its profound teachings, the Gita continues to inspire individuals worldwide to lead meaningful lives, cultivate spiritual awareness, and strive for inner harmony and peace. The enduring popularity and influence of the Bhagavad Gita underscore its significance as a spiritual and philosophical masterpiece that transcends cultural boundaries and resonates with the deepest aspirations of humanity.

Key Philosophical Concepts in the Bhagavad Gita

At the outset, it needs to be well understood that Gita is not just a religious work but covers a wide spectrum of topics such as philosophy, physics, psychology, sociology, culture, nature, history, tradition, belief, reason, and religion.

Dharma and Duty - In Hindu philosophy, 'dharma' encompasses various meanings, including duty, righteousness, moral law, and ethical conduct. It refers to the inherent nature or essence of things and individuals, as well as the principles that sustain and uphold the universe.

Dharma guides individuals in living harmoniously within society and fulfilling their roles and responsibilities with integrity and righteousness. The Bhagavad Gita addresses the concept of duty (*Swadharma*) within the context of one's prescribed roles and responsibilities in life. Arjuna, a warrior prince, faces a moral dilemma on the battlefield where he must fight against his relatives, teachers, and friends. His reluctance to engage in the battle stems from ethical concerns about the consequences of his actions. Krishna, acting as Arjuna's charioteer and spiritual guide, imparts wisdom on the nature of dharma and duty. He advises Arjuna that as a warrior (*Kshatriya*), it is his duty to engage in battle, emphasizing the importance of fulfilling one's responsibilities without attachment to personal desires or outcomes. Krishna states (BG 3.30):

मयि सर्वाणि कर्माणि संन्यस्याध्यात्मचेतसा
निराशीर्निर्ममो भूत्वा युध्यस्व विगतज्वर: ॥ ३० ॥

(Therefore, O Arjuna, surrendering all your works unto Me, with full knowledge of Me, without desires for profit, with no claims to proprietorship, and free from grief and lethargy, fight."-BG 3.30).

This teaching emphasizes on the principle that performing one's duties selflessly and with dedication is essential for spiritual growth and societal harmony. The concept of dharma in the Bhagavad Gita emphasizes ethical conduct in all aspects of life. It advocates for righteous action (dharmic karma) that is in accordance with moral principles and universal laws. Krishna teaches Arjuna that by adhering to his dharma as a warrior, he contributes to the preservation of order (rta) and justice (dharma) in the world. The teachings on dharma and duty in the Bhagavad Gita are not confined to specific roles or professions but apply universally to all individuals. It emphasizes that everyone has a unique set of duties (svadharma) based on their inherent qualities (guna) and station in life (varna). By performing these duties conscientiously and without attachment to personal gain, individuals contribute to the welfare of society and their spiritual evolution. The Bhagavad Gita integrates the concept of dharma with other paths to spiritual realization, such as Karma Yoga (the yoga of selfless action), Bhakti Yoga (the yoga of devotion), and Jnana Yoga (the yoga of knowledge). These paths are complementary and support individuals in aligning their actions, thoughts, and emotions with higher spiritual principles. In contemporary society, the concept of dharma and duty as discussed in the Bhagavad Gita holds profound relevance. It offers insights into ethical decision-making, personal responsibility, and the importance of integrity in professional and personal life. By embracing one's dharma and fulfilling duties conscientiously, individuals can contribute positively to their communities and lead meaningful lives.

The philosophical concept of 'dharma and duty' in the Bhagavad Gita serves as a guiding principle for ethical conduct, righteous action, and spiritual fulfilment. It emphasizes the importance of fulfilling one's responsibilities (*karma*) without attachment to outcomes, thereby fostering harmony and balance in both individual lives and society at large. The teachings of the Gita transcend time and cultural boundaries, offering timeless wisdom that continues to inspire and guide spiritual seekers and ethical practitioners worldwide. Through its profound insights into dharma, the Bhagavad Gita encourages individuals to align their actions with moral principles, uphold righteousness, and strive for personal and collective well-being. Its enduring legacy underlines its significance as a philosophical and spiritual masterpiece that continues to illuminate the path to self-realization and spiritual liberation.

Karma Yoga – the path of selfless action

कर्मण्येवाधिकारस्ते मा फलेषु कदाचन
मा कर्मफलहेतुर्भूर्मा ते सङ्गोऽस्त्वकर्मणि ॥ ४७ ॥

("You have a right to perform your prescribed duties, but you are not entitled to the fruits of your actions. Never consider yourself to be the cause of the results of your activities, nor be attached to inaction. BG 2.47")

Karma Yoga, as explained in the Bhagavad Gita, emphasizes the performance of one's duties and actions without attachment to outcomes or personal gains. It is rooted in the idea of selfless service (seva) and the belief that one's actions should be dedicated to a higher purpose, such as spiritual growth or the well-being of society. Central to Karma Yoga is the principle of performing actions without attachment to their fruits. Lord Krishna advises Arjuna that it is not the results of actions that should motivate him, but the duty itself. This detachment from outcomes liberates individuals from anxiety, ego, and the dualities of success and failure. Dharma, often translated as duty or righteousness, is another foundational concept in Karma Yoga. Each individual is born with specific responsibilities (svadharma) based on their nature, role, and station in life. By fulfilling one's duties sincerely and selflessly, individuals contribute to the harmony and order of society. Karma Yoga is considered a path to spiritual liberation (moksha) through disciplined action. By purifying the mind and dedicating one's actions to the divine or to the greater good, individuals transcend the cycle of birth and death (sansara) and attain union with the ultimate reality (Brahman). The teachings of Karma Yoga extend beyond ancient scripture and offer practical wisdom for contemporary life. Karma Yoga highlights the importance of ethical conduct and integrity in all aspects of life. By acting selflessly and responsibly, individuals contribute positively to their communities and cultivate virtues such as compassion, honesty, and humility (ethical living). Practicing Karma Yoga requires mindfulness in action—being fully present and conscious of one's intentions and the impact of one's actions on others. This mindfulness fosters a deeper connection to the present moment and promotes inner peace and harmony. Through Karma Yoga, individuals develop a sense of purpose and fulfilment by aligning their actions with their values and higher ideals. By transcending personal desires and ego, they experience inner growth and spiritual evolution. While Karma Yoga emphasizes selfless action, critics argue that it may be impractical in certain modern contexts where outcomes are critical, such as in business or politics. However, proponents argue that even in such contexts, focusing on ethical conduct and the well-being of others can lead to more sustainable and harmonious outcomes. The philosophical concept of Karma Yoga in the Bhagavad Gita offers profound insights into the nature of human action, duty, and spiritual growth. By advocating selfless action and detachment from outcomes, Karma Yoga provides a pathway to ethical living, personal fulfilment, and spiritual liberation. Its timeless teachings continue to resonate with seekers of truth and wisdom, transcending cultural and temporal boundaries to inspire individuals toward a life of purpose and service. In essence, Karma Yoga invites individuals to not only perform their duties diligently but to do so with a sense of devotion and selflessness, thereby transforming their actions into a means of spiritual elevation and union with the divine.

Bhakti Yoga – the path of devotion

One of the central teachings Krishna imparts is the path of Bhakti Yoga, the yoga of devotion. Bhakti Yoga stands out among the various paths of yoga due to its emphasis on love, devotion, and surrender to the divine. At its core, Bhakti Yoga revolves around love and devotion to a personal deity or the formless divine. The Gita describes Bhakti Yoga as a path accessible to all, irrespective of social status or intellectual capacity. It is characterized by unwavering faith and the heartfelt yearning for union with the divine. Krishna explains in Chapter 9, Verse 22 of the Gita:

अनन्याश्चिन्तयन्तो मां ये जना: पर्युपासते
तेषां नित्याभियुक्तानां योगक्षेमं वहाम्यहम्

(those who always worship Me with exclusive devotion, meditating on My transcendental form – to them whose minds are always absorbed in me, I carry what they lack, and I preserve what they possess - BG 9.22.)

This verse underscores the importance of sincere devotion and love as the means to attain spiritual realization and closeness to the divine. Central to Bhakti Yoga is the concept of surrender (prapatti) to the divine will. Practitioners surrender their ego, desires, and actions to their chosen deity or the supreme reality (Brahman). This surrender is not passive but involves active engagement in loving service (seva) and devotion. Krishna emphasizes in Chapter 18, Verse 66:

सर्वधर्मान्परित्यज्य मामेकं शरणं व्रज
अहं त्वां सर्वपापेभ्यो मोक्षयिष्यामि मा शुचः

(Abandon all varieties of dharmas and simply surrender unto Me alone. I shall liberate you from all sinful reactions; do not fear-BG 18.66)

Here, surrender is portrayed as the ultimate path to liberation (moksha), freeing the practitioner from the cycle of birth and death (sansara). Bhakti Yoga teaches the importance of cultivating virtues such as humility, compassion, and patience. These virtues are seen as natural outcomes of deep devotion and love for the divine, fostering a harmonious relationship not only with the divine but also with fellow beings and the world at large.

Bhakti Yoga encompasses a range of practices aimed at deepening one's devotion and love for the divine. These practices are accessible to individuals from all walks of life and include singing devotional songs (bhajans) and chanting the names and attributes of the divine (kirtan) to invoke a sense of divine presence and connection, Performing worship rituals (puja) with deep reverence and love, offering flowers, incense, and food to the deity as acts of devotion, Repetition of the divine name or mantra (japa) as a means of focusing the mind and cultivating a sense of intimacy with the divine, Studying sacred texts such as the Bhagavad Gita, Ramayana, and Puranas to deepen understanding and knowledge of the divine, and Selfless service (seva) performed with humility and love, recognizing the divine presence in all beings and serving them as an act of devotion.

Bhakti Yoga holds immense significance in the spiritual journey of an individual. Unlike other paths of yoga that may require rigorous intellectual inquiry (Jnana Yoga), discipline and self-control (Raja Yoga), or selfless action (Karma Yoga), Bhakti Yoga emphasizes the power of love and devotion as a transformative force. It is considered the most direct and joyful path to realizing one's true nature and attaining union with the divine. Bhakti Yoga is inclusive and universal, transcending barriers of caste, creed, and gender. It emphasizes the underlying unity of all existence and encourages individuals to see the divine in everyone and everything. This universality makes Bhakti Yoga particularly relevant in today's world, promoting harmony, compassion, and tolerance. The practice of Bhakti Yoga also brings emotional fulfilment and inner peace. By cultivating a loving relationship with the divine, practitioners experience a profound sense of contentment, regardless of external circumstances. This emotional fulfilment not only enhances personal well-being but also radiates outwards, positively influencing relationships and communities. To summarise, Bhakti Yoga as propounded in the Bhagavad Gita is a path of love, devotion, and surrender to the divine. It offers a practical and inclusive approach to spirituality, emphasizing the power of heartfelt devotion, selfless service, and unwavering faith. Through practices such as chanting, worship, and selfless service, practitioners of Bhakti Yoga cultivate a deep and personal relationship with the divine, leading to spiritual growth, emotional fulfilment, and ultimately, liberation from the cycle of birth and death.

Jnana Yoga – the path of knowledge

Jnana Yoga stands out as the path of knowledge, emphasizing discernment, wisdom, and self-realization. Rooted in the pursuit of true knowledge and understanding of the self and the universe, Jnana Yoga as discussed in the Bhagavad Gita offers seekers a rigorous intellectual and philosophical approach to spiritual growth. Jnana Yoga is characterized by its emphasis on discerning the eternal and impermanent aspects of existence. At its core lies the understanding of the self (atman) as distinct from the temporary material world (Prakriti). The Bhagavad Gita, through the teachings of Lord Krishna to Arjuna, reveals this principle of discernment and knowledge. In Chapter 2, Verse 11, Krishna addresses Arjuna:

अशोच्यानन्वशोचस्त्वं प्रज्ञावादांश्च भाषसे
गतासूनगतासूंश्च नानुशोचन्ति पण्डिता:

(You are mourning for those who should not be mourned for, and yet you speak words of wisdom. The wise do not grieve for the dead or for the living – BG 2.11)

This verse highlights Krishna's instruction to Arjuna to transcend his identification with the impermanent body and recognize the eternal nature of the soul (atman). Jnana Yoga teaches that true knowledge leads to liberation (moksha) by unravelling the illusion (Maya) of material existence and revealing the eternal truth of the self. Another key principle of Jnana Yoga is the importance of self-inquiry (vichara) and introspection. Practitioners are encouraged to question the nature of reality, the self, and the ultimate truth. Through deep contemplation and reflection, one gains insight into the underlying unity of existence and transcends dualistic thinking. This process of self-inquiry is exemplified in Chapter 4, Verse 38:

न हि ज्ञानेन सदृशं पवित्रमिह विद्यते |
तत्स्वयं योगसंसिद्ध: कालेनात्मनि विन्दति || 38||

(In this world, there is nothing as purifying as divine knowledge. One who has attained purity of mind through prolonged practice of Yog, receives such knowledge within the heart, in due course of time).

Here, knowledge (jnana) is extolled as the ultimate purifier, leading to self-realization and spiritual perfection. Jnana Yoga emphasizes the cultivation of qualities such as humility, detachment, and equanimity. These virtues are considered essential for gaining true knowledge and overcoming the egoic tendencies that obscure the perception of reality. By relinquishing attachment to transient phenomena and identifying with the eternal self, practitioners attain inner peace and spiritual freedom. Jnana Yoga employs various practices aimed at cultivating wisdom, discernment, and self-realization. These practices are designed to refine intellect, deepen understanding, and facilitate the direct experience of spiritual truths. Key practices include studying scriptures such as the Bhagavad Gita, Upanishads, and Vedanta texts to gain knowledge of philosophical principles and spiritual truths. Texts like the Gita offer profound insights into the nature of existence, the self, and the path to liberation, engaging in introspective practices to question the nature of the self, the source of consciousness, and the underlying unity of all existence. This inquiry leads to the dissolution of false identifications and the realization of one's true nature, cultivating inner stillness and focused awareness through meditation practices. Meditation enhances clarity of mind, deepens contemplative insight, and fosters direct experience of spiritual truths beyond intellectual understanding, developing discernment to distinguish between the eternal and transient aspects of existence. Discrimination helps practitioners overcome ignorance (avidya) and align their actions with spiritual principles and seek the company of wise teachers (gurus) and fellow seekers who embody spiritual wisdom. Satsang facilitates learning, inspiration, and guidance on the path of Jnana Yoga.

Jnana Yoga holds profound significance in the spiritual journey of individuals seeking self-realization and liberation from the cycle of birth and death. Unlike other paths of yoga that may emphasize devotion (Bhakti Yoga), selfless action (Karma Yoga), or meditation (Raja Yoga),

Jnana Yoga focuses on intellectual inquiry and the pursuit of knowledge as a means to transcendental realization. By unravelling the nature of the self and discerning the underlying unity of existence, practitioners of Jnana Yoga attain a profound sense of freedom, peace, and inner fulfilment. This knowledge-based approach fosters intellectual clarity, emotional equanimity, and spiritual maturity, enabling individuals to navigate life's challenges with wisdom and detachment. Jnana Yoga promotes the integration of spiritual insights into daily life, fostering harmony, compassion, and ethical conduct. The realization of one's true nature as pure consciousness (Brahman) leads to a deep-seated sense of harmony with all beings and the universe, transcending divisive boundaries of ego and identity. Jnana Yoga as propounded in the Bhagavad Gita offers seekers a path of intellectual inquiry, discernment, and self-realization. Through the cultivation of wisdom, discrimination, and introspection, practitioners of Jnana Yoga unravel the illusion of material existence and attain liberation from suffering and ignorance. The teachings of the Gita inspire individuals to engage in self-inquiry, study of scriptures, meditation, and association with wise teachers to deepen their understanding of the self and the ultimate truth. Jnana Yoga stands as a beacon of intellectual rigor and spiritual insight, guiding seekers on the transformative journey toward enlightenment and union with the divine. By embodying the principles of discernment, knowledge, and self-realization, practitioners of Jnana Yoga fulfil the highest aspirations of human life—realizing the eternal truth and attaining spiritual liberation.

Dhyana Yoga – the path of meditation

Dhyana Yoga, often referred to as the yoga of meditation, occupies a central place. Rooted in the practice of cultivating inner stillness, focused awareness, and transcendent states of consciousness, Dhyana Yoga as described in the Bhagavad Gita offers seekers a systematic approach to attain union with the divine. Dhyana Yoga emphasizes the cultivation of meditation as a means to quiet the mind, attain inner peace, and experience higher states of consciousness. The Bhagavad Gita describes meditation as a transformative practice that enables the practitioner to transcend the limitations of the ego and perceive the divine essence within and beyond oneself. In Chapter 6, Verse 10, Lord Krishna instructs Arjuna:

योगी युञ्जीत सततमात्मानं रहसि स्थित:
एकाकी यतचित्तात्मा निराशीरपरिग्रह:

(Those who seek the state of Yog should reside in seclusion, constantly engaged in meditation with a controlled mind and body, getting rid of desires and possessions for enjoyment and fixing the mind on me).

Here, Krishna emphasizes the importance of concentration (Dharana) and withdrawing the mind from external distractions to focus on the divine. Dhyana Yoga teaches that through the sustained practice of meditation, one can achieve union (yoga) with the divine consciousness (Brahman) and realize the true nature of the self (atman). Another key principle of Dhyana Yoga is the cultivation of inner awareness and mindfulness. Practitioners are encouraged to develop heightened sensitivity to their thoughts, emotions, and sensations, cultivating a state of detached observation (Sakshi Bhava). This mindfulness facilitates self-awareness and insight into the workings of the mind, leading to greater clarity and understanding. Dhyana Yoga emphasizes the integration of meditative awareness into daily life. Meditation is not merely a practice confined to a specific time or place but a continuous state of consciousness that permeates all activities. By cultivating mindfulness and presence, practitioners deepen their connection with the divine and align their actions with spiritual principles. Dhyana Yoga employs various practices aimed at developing concentration, stilling the mind, and deepening meditative awareness. These practices are designed to cultivate inner peace, spiritual insight, and union with the divine. Engaging in physical postures (asanas) and breath control techniques (pranayama) to prepare the body and mind for meditation. Asanas help cultivate physical stability and comfort, while pranayama regulates the breath and enhances vitality, facilitating focused attention during meditation. Practicing concentration techniques to focus the mind on a single point or object (such as a mantra, image, or the breath). Dharana strengthens mental discipline and prepares the mind for deeper states of meditation (dhyana). Cultivating sustained attention and inner stillness through meditation practices. Dhyana involves maintaining uninterrupted awareness of the chosen object or focal point, gradually transcending dualistic thinking, and experiencing states of expanded consciousness. Chanting sacred sounds or repetitive phrases (mantras) to induce a state of deep concentration and inner resonance. Mantra meditation harmonizes the mind and facilitates the absorption of consciousness into higher spiritual orbits. Engaging in introspective practices to study scriptures, contemplate spiritual teachings, and reflect on the nature of the self. Svadhyaya deepens understanding and insight, fostering intellectual clarity and spiritual growth.

Dhyana Yoga holds profound significance in the spiritual journey of individuals seeking self-realization and union with the divine. Unlike other paths of yoga that may emphasize devotion (Bhakti Yoga), selfless action (Karma Yoga), or intellectual inquiry (Jnana Yoga), Dhyana Yoga focuses on cultivating inner stillness, heightened awareness, and direct experience of transcendental states of consciousness.

By practicing meditation, practitioners of Dhyana Yoga purify the mind, dissolve mental obstacles, and attain inner peace. Meditation fosters equanimity, emotional stability, and resilience in the face of life's challenges, enabling individuals to navigate worldly responsibilities with clarity and detachment. Dhyana Yoga also facilitates the direct experience of spiritual truths and the realization of one's essential nature as pure consciousness (atman). Through sustained meditation practice, practitioners transcend egoic limitations and merge their individual awareness with the universal consciousness (Brahman), experiencing profound unity and harmony with all beings.

Dhyana Yoga as propounded in the Bhagavad Gita offers seekers a transformative path of meditation, inner stillness, and spiritual awakening. Through the cultivation of concentration, mindfulness, and meditative awareness, practitioners of Dhyana Yoga attain union with the divine consciousness and realize the eternal truth of the self. The teachings of the Gita inspire individuals to engage in regular meditation practice, embodying the principles of inner peace, spiritual insight, and self-transcendence. By integrating Dhyana Yoga into their daily lives, seekers cultivate profound spiritual growth, emotional well-being, and alignment with the divine purpose. Dhyana Yoga stands as a timeless path of meditation and self-discovery, guiding seekers on the transformative journey towards enlightenment, inner freedom, and union with the divine. As humanity continues to seek meaning and fulfilment in an ever-changing world, the principles of Dhyana Yoga offer a profound pathway to spiritual realization and ultimate liberation.

Raja Yoga – the path of discipline

Raja Yoga, also known as the Royal Yoga or the Yoga of Meditation, occupies a significant place. Rooted in the practice of mental discipline, self-control, and meditative absorption, Raja Yoga as described in the Bhagavad Gita offers seekers a systematic approach to attain union with the divine. Raja Yoga is characterized by its emphasis on mental discipline, control of the mind, and cultivation of meditative absorption (samadhi). The Bhagavad Gita delineates the principles of Raja Yoga through the teachings of Lord Krishna to Arjuna, emphasizing the importance of mastering the mind to attain spiritual liberation. In Chapter 6 Verse 35, Krishna says:

असंशयं महाबाहो मनो दुर्निग्रहं चलम्
अभ्यासेन तु कौन्तेय वैराग्येण च गृह्यते

(O mighty-armed son of Kunti, the mind is indeed exceedingly difficult to restrain. But by practice and detachment, it can be controlled). This verse underscores the challenge of controlling the restless mind (chitta), which is essential for progressing on the path of Raja Yoga. Krishna advises Arjuna that through disciplined practice (abhyasa) and detachment (vairagya), one can achieve mastery over the mind and attain inner peace. Another key principle of Raja Yoga is the practice of the eightfold path (ashtanga yoga) as detailed by the sage Patanjali in his Yoga Sutras. These eight limbs include ethical guidelines (yamas and niyamas), physical postures (asanas), breath control (pranayama), sensory withdrawal (pratyahara), concentration (dharana), meditation (dhyana), and absorption (samadhi). The Bhagavad Gita aligns with these principles, emphasizing the systematic progression through these stages to attain union with the divine consciousness (Brahman). Raja Yoga emphasizes the cultivation of virtues such as discipline, perseverance, and equanimity. Practitioners are encouraged to lead a disciplined life, adhering to moral principles, and cultivating inner harmony. Through the practice of mental control and meditative absorption, practitioners attain spiritual maturity and transcend the fluctuations of the mind.

Raja Yoga employs systematic practices aimed at purifying the mind, cultivating mental focus, and attaining meditative absorption. These practices are designed to facilitate inner transformation, spiritual awakening, and union with the divine. Raja prescribes engaging in stable and comfortable physical postures to promote physical health, mental clarity, and energetic balance. Asanas prepare the body and mind for prolonged periods of meditation and facilitate the flow of prana (vital energy) through the energy channels (nadis), practicing conscious regulation of the breath to expand lung capacity, increase vital energy, and calm the mind. Pranayama techniques synchronize breath with movement, promoting relaxation, concentration, and heightened awareness, withdrawing the senses from external stimuli and redirecting attention inward. Pratyahara facilitates mental focus, minimizes distractions, and prepares the mind for deeper stages of meditation, cultivating a single-pointed focus on a chosen object or mental image (such as a candle flame, mantra, or deity). Dharana enhances mental clarity, strengthens concentration, and prepares the mind for meditation (dhyana), cultivating sustained and uninterrupted awareness of the chosen object or focal point. Dhyana involves effortless concentration, inner stillness, and absorption in the present moment, leading to heightened states of consciousness and spiritual insight and attaining a state of profound meditative absorption where the meditator merges with the object of meditation or experiences union with the divine consciousness. Samadhi transcends duality and egoic limitations, leading to a direct experience of spiritual reality and ultimate liberation (moksha). Raja Yoga holds profound significance in the spiritual journey of individuals seeking self-realization, inner peace, and union with the divine. Unlike other paths of yoga that may emphasize devotion (Bhakti Yoga), selfless action (Karma Yoga), or intellectual inquiry (Jnana Yoga), Raja Yoga focuses on systematic practices of mental control, meditation, and spiritual absorption.

By practicing Raja Yoga, practitioners purify the mind, cultivate inner stillness, and attain meditative absorption. Meditation practices enhance mental clarity, emotional stability, and spiritual insight, enabling individuals to transcend egoic limitations and experience higher states of consciousness. Moreover, Raja Yoga facilitates the direct experience of spiritual truths and the realization of one's essential nature as pure consciousness (atman). Through the systematic cultivation of the eightfold path, practitioners align their thoughts, actions, and aspirations with spiritual principles, fostering inner harmony, and spiritual growth.

Raja Yoga as propounded in the Bhagavad Gita offers seekers a transformative path of mental discipline, meditation, and spiritual realization. Through the systematic practice of Ashtanga yoga, practitioners purify the mind, cultivate inner peace, and attain union with the divine consciousness. The teachings of the Gita inspire individuals to engage in the regular practice of Raja Yoga, embodying the principles of discipline, concentration, and meditative absorption. By integrating Raja Yoga into their daily lives, seekers cultivate profound spiritual growth, emotional well-being, and alignment with the divine purpose. Raja Yoga stands as a timeless path of meditation and self-discovery, guiding seekers on the transformative journey towards enlightenment, inner freedom, and union with the divine. As humanity continues to seek meaning and fulfilment in an ever-changing world, the principles of Raja Yoga offer a profound pathway to spiritual realization and ultimate liberation.

Abhyasa Yoga – the path of practice

Abhyasa Yoga stands out as the yoga of diligent practice and disciplined effort. Rooted in the principles of persistent effort, self-discipline, and dedication to spiritual practice, Abhyasa Yoga as elaborated in the Bhagavad Gita offers seekers a systematic approach to attain union with the divine. This passage explores the philosophical foundations of Abhyasa Yoga, elucidating its key principles, practices, and significance in the journey towards spiritual enlightenment. Abhyasa Yoga emphasizes the importance of disciplined effort and consistent practice as essential components of spiritual growth and self-realization. The Bhagavad Gita delineates the principles of Abhyasa Yoga through the teachings of Lord Krishna to Arjuna, highlighting the transformative power of persistent practice and dedicated effort.

Verse BG 6.35 cited above also underscores the challenge of mastering the restless mind (chitta) and the necessity of disciplined practice (abhyasa) to achieve mental control and spiritual progress. Krishna advises Arjuna that through sustained effort and detachment from worldly distractions, one can cultivate inner peace and spiritual realization. Another key principle of Abhyasa Yoga is the cultivation of self-discipline (tapas) and determination (Sankalpa). Practitioners are encouraged to lead a disciplined life, adhering to ethical guidelines (yamas and niyamas), and dedicating themselves wholeheartedly to spiritual practices. By cultivating determination and perseverance, individuals overcome obstacles on the spiritual path and achieve steady progress toward self-realization. Furthermore, Abhyasa Yoga emphasizes the importance of regularity and continuity in spiritual practice. Practitioners engage in daily rituals, routines, and practices that reinforce spiritual discipline and foster inner transformation. Through consistent effort and dedicated practice, individuals gradually purify the mind, cultivate virtues, and align their actions with spiritual principles. Abhyasa Yoga employs various practices aimed at cultivating disciplined effort, steady progress, and spiritual transformation. These practices are designed to develop inner strength, resilience, and unwavering commitment to the path of self-realization. These practices include engaging in daily rituals, routines, and practices that promote physical health, mental clarity, and spiritual growth. Sadhana includes practices such as meditation, mantra chanting, prayer, self-inquiry, and study of sacred texts (Svadhyaya), cultivating inner stillness, focused awareness, and meditative absorption through regular practice. Meditation enhances mental clarity, emotional stability, and spiritual insight, enabling practitioners to transcend egoic limitations and experience higher states of consciousness, practicing physical postures (asanas) and breath control techniques (pranayama) to harmonize the body, mind, and energy channels (Nadis). Asanas and pranayama enhance vitality, increase concentration, and prepare the practitioner for deeper stages of meditation, engaging in introspective practices to examine one's thoughts, emotions, beliefs, and actions. Self-reflection fosters self-awareness, clarity of purpose, and alignment with spiritual values, guiding practitioners on the path of self-realization and performing selfless service (karma yoga) and acts of compassion to cultivate humility, generosity, and spiritual maturity. Service is seen as an expression of devotion and an opportunity to transcend egoic desires, contributing to the welfare of others and the harmony of the universe.

Abhyasa Yoga holds profound significance in the spiritual journey of individuals seeking self-realization, inner peace, and union with the divine. Unlike other paths of yoga that may emphasize devotion (Bhakti Yoga), intellectual inquiry (Jnana Yoga), or meditation (Raja Yoga), Abhyasa Yoga focuses on disciplined effort, persistent practice, and gradual spiritual evolution. By engaging in regular practice and cultivating self-discipline, practitioners of Abhyasa Yoga purify the mind, strengthen their resolve, and align their actions with spiritual principles. Abhyasa Yoga instils virtues such as perseverance, resilience, and inner strength, enabling individuals to overcome challenges on the spiritual path and achieve lasting transformation. Abhyasa Yoga fosters a sense of commitment and dedication to spiritual growth, guiding practitioners toward self-realization and ultimate liberation (moksha). Through disciplined effort and steady progress, individuals deepen their understanding of the self, transcend egoic limitations, and experience unity with the divine consciousness (Brahman).

Abhyasa Yoga as propounded in the Bhagavad Gita offers seekers a transformative path of disciplined effort, dedicated practice, and spiritual realization. Through the cultivation of self-discipline, determination, and regularity in spiritual practice, practitioners of Abhyasa Yoga purify the mind, cultivate virtues, and align their lives with spiritual principles. The teachings of the Gita inspire individuals to engage in the consistent practice of Abhyasa Yoga, embodying the principles of disciplined effort, perseverance, and unwavering commitment. By integrating Abhyasa Yoga into their daily lives, seekers cultivate profound spiritual growth, inner peace, and alignment with the divine purpose. It stands as a timeless path of diligent practice and self-discovery, guiding seekers on the transformative journey towards enlightenment, inner freedom, and union with the divine. As humanity continues to seek meaning and fulfilment in an ever-changing world, the principles of Abhyasa Yoga offer a profound pathway to spiritual realization and ultimate liberation.

We have now examined the socio-political and cultural ambience in which the Dnyaneshwari and Gita Rahasya are situated and also developed an understanding of the philosophical foundations of the original text, Bhagavad Gita. We shall now, in the next chapter, attempt to undertake a comparative analysis of the philosophical perspectives of Sant Dnyaneshwar and Lokmanya Bal Gangadhar Tilak as portrayed in their interpretations of Bhagavad Gita.

Author's Notes:

One of the landmark contributions to the study of the Mahabharata which I had an opportunity to read has been 'Yuganta" by Iravati Karve. It offers a bold and insightful critique that challenges the conventional readings of the epic. While doing so, it also offers a deeper and critical analysis of the Mahabharata. Karve, an anthropologist, and sociologist, brings her unique perspective to her examination, blending rigorous scholarly research with a deep understanding of human nature and societal structures.

Karve's dissection of the key characters is one of the standout features. Looking at the epic through the lens of each of these characters is a literary delight. She boldly, strips away their mythological grandeur and reveals human vulnerabilities and complexities and in the process succeeds in bringing the characters to life and making them identifiable. For instance, she highlights Draupadi as a strong, assertive woman navigating a patriarchal world, which provides a refreshing contrast to traditional depictions. Her analysis sheds light on the intersection of mythology and history, suggesting that the Mahabharata serves as a repository of ancient Indian wisdom and a commentary on its society. Unlike many traditional interpretations that glorify the epic's heroes and their actions, Karve adopts a critical stance, questioning the morality and motivations of the characters.

Yuganta, to me, is a remarkable example of how history should be comprehended. Yuganta remains an essential read for anyone interested in exploring Mahabharata through a critical and contemporary lens.

References

(Iravati Karve, Yuganta, 1967)

Chapter 3

Comparative Analysis of Philosophical Perspectives

Reconciling the transcendent and rational approaches to Bhagavad Gita

भूमिरापोऽनलो वायुः खं मनो बुद्धिरेव च ।
अहंकार इतीयं मे भिन्ना प्रकृतिरष्टधा ॥ ४ ॥
या आठांची जे साम्यावस्था । ते माझी परम प्रकृति पार्था ।
तिये नाम व्यवस्था । जीवु ऐसी ॥ १९ ॥

(Earth, water, fire, air, ether, mind, understanding, and self-intellect, are the eight elements of my nature. The equilibrium between these eight elements is My higher nature, O Partha, and is called the life element.)

Two significant philosophical perspectives emerge from the interpretations of Bhagavad Gita by Sant Dnyaneshwar and Lokmanya

Tilak, each offering unique insights shaped by their respective contexts and philosophical frameworks. Dnyaneshwar, approached the Gita with a mystico-philosophical lens, emphasizing the path of devotion (Bhakti Yoga) and the significance of divine grace in spiritual liberation. In contrast, Tilak, interpreted the Gita through a socio-political and nationalist perspective, highlighting its teachings on duty (Karma Yoga) and selfless action as fundamental for individual and societal upliftment. A comparative analysis of their interpretations not only reveals their distinct philosophical orientations but also sheds light on how the timeless wisdom of the Gita resonates across diverse intellectual and cultural landscapes in India.

Comparative study of the fundamental philosophical approach to Bhagavad Gita

It is here at the very beginning that I shall dispel this popular notion that Dnyaneshwari is (solely) a mystical text. Portraying it to be mystical would undermine this remarkable philosophical treatise that addresses various aspects of life, ethics, and nature of reality and engages with complex ideas about the self, the universe and the divine. Its philosophical framework firmly grounded in vedantas, social context that responds to the social issues of its time, literary merit that invites diverse interpretations through use of imagery and metaphors, practical guidance for living a virtuous life and interconnectedness of thought which links Indian philosophy with spirituality makes it an exemplary work that speaks to both the heart and the intellect.

Central to Dnyaneshwari is the theme of Bhakti Yoga, the path of loving devotion to God. Dnyaneshwar approaches the Bhagavad Gita through the lens of Bhakti. A reading of Dnyaneshwari will make one realise that contrary to popular notions surrounding the Bhakti movement, Dnyaneshwar possessed a profound understanding of metaphysical monism, recognizing it as the foundational principle that underpinned the spiritual awakening of the era and in that Dnyaneshwari can also be comprehended as a philosophical treatise. He emphasizes that true knowledge (jnana) arises from a heart filled with devotion as much as it does with an intellectual understanding. He portrays Lord Krishna as the Supreme Being who incarnates to guide humanity towards spiritual liberation through unwavering devotion and surrender. Dnyaneshwari emphasizes on the importance of surrendering one's ego and desires to the divine will (Ishwara prapatti). He interprets Krishna's teachings on surrender as the essence of spiritual practice, where the seeker relinquishes personal attachments and surrenders completely to divine grace. Through surrender, one transcends the limitations of the ego and attains union (yoga) with the Supreme Self (Brahman). Dnyaneshwar integrates various paths to spiritual realization, emphasizing the harmony between Bhakti Yoga, Karma Yoga (selfless action), and Jnana Yoga (knowledge). He presents an integrated approach where devotion, selfless action, and self-inquiry converge to lead the seeker toward spiritual awakening and union with the divine.

Tilak's lens is that of action. Tilak emphasized Karma Yoga, the path of selfless action performed without attachment to results, as a means to fulfil one's duty (dharma) towards society and nation. He interpreted Krishna's teachings on duty and righteous action (Karma Yoga) in the Gita to motivate individuals towards national service and social reform. Unlike Dnyaneshwar's focus on devotion and spiritual liberation, Tilak's interpretation of the Gita was infused with a nationalist ideology. He viewed Krishna as a symbol of righteous action and national duty, advocating for selfless service to the country as a form of spiritual practice. Tilak's interpretation of the Gita, particularly in Gita Rahasya, emphasized the practical application of spiritual principles in everyday life and social governance. He sought to mobilize the masses through the teachings of the Gita, inspiring them to rise against oppression and work towards national regeneration.

Distinct motivations in the study and interpretation of Bhagavad Gita

Dnyaneshwar was born into a family of scholars and saints in Maharashtra. From an immature age, he exhibited a deep inclination towards spiritual pursuits and a thirst for knowledge. His early initiation into the Nath tradition of yoga and meditation provided him with a foundation in spiritual practices that emphasized direct experience and inner realization. The Bhagavad Gita held a special significance for Dnyaneshwar as he saw it not only as a religious text but also as a profound philosophical treatise that encapsulated the essence of spiritual wisdom and ethical principles. One of Dnyaneshwar's principal motivations behind writing Dnyaneshwari was to take the teachings of Bhagavad Gita to the common people, especially those who did not have access to Sanskrit texts or lacked formal education. Dnyaneshwar endeavoured to liberate the common people from restrictive cultural norms, traditions or systems that limited their expression, identity, or agency. Through this Dnyaneshwari, he perhaps undertook a cultural emancipation that was aimed at creating a more equitable and open society. This is also the reason Dnyaneshwari is written in Marathi. Dnyaneshwar's work was also motivated by a desire to reform the societal and religious practices of his time. He sought to challenge rigid orthodoxy and caste-based discrimination, promoting a message of universal love, compassion, and spiritual equality through his writings and teachings.

Bal Gangadhar Tilak said that he began studying the Bhagavad Gita because he was told that it contained the Hindu religion's principles and philosophy, and he wanted to find answers to the questions lingering in his mind. As a child, Tilak was made to understand that the core teaching of the Hindu religion was freeing oneself from worldly existence and surrendering to the divine to achieve liberation (moksha). Tilak's intellect gave rise to several queries about the inherent contradictions in this preaching that caused one to sacrifice the world in which one was born. Tilak turned to the Bhagavad Gita to resolve this dilemma. In due course, Tilak began to believe that the Gita provided a strong justification for activism, which conflicted with the mainstream views of the time. To support his views, Tilak wrote his interpretations of the Gita basing his thesis on the Mimansa rule of interpretation and used commentary by Ramanuja, as well as his translation of the Gita. Tilak's motivation behind writing the Gita Rahasya was driven by a synthesis of spiritual inquiry, nationalist fervour, and a commitment to interpreting and popularizing the timeless wisdom of the Bhagavad Gita for the benefit of his fellow countrymen. His work continues to be studied and appreciated not only for its historical significance but also for its enduring philosophical insights into the complexities of human existence and societal transformation.

Philosophical themes and interpretations

Atman (Self)

Dnyaneshwari interprets the Atman as the eternal, indivisible essence of the individual, distinct yet inseparable from the Supreme Brahman. According to Dnyaneshwar, the Atman is not bound by the limitations of the physical body but is eternal, infinite, and part of the cosmic consciousness (Brahman). Through his commentary, he emphasizes the unity of the individual soul (Jivatma) with the universal soul (Paramatma), advocating a path of devotion (Bhakti) and self-realization.

In contrast, Gita Rahasya by Tilak explores the concept of Atman in the context of national duty and social responsibility. For Tilak, the Atman embodies the spirit of sacrifice and selflessness, essential qualities in the struggle for national liberation and social reform. Tilak interprets the Atman as the essence of individual agency and moral responsibility, emphasizing Gita's teachings on Karma Yoga and the performance of one's duty without attachment to the results.

Self-Realisation (Moksha)

Dnyaneshwari emphasizes the path of Bhakti (devotion) as a means to realize the true nature of the self and attain liberation (Moksha). According to Dnyaneshwar, devotion to the divine (Bhagavan) through prayer, meditation, and surrender leads to the dissolution of ego and the realization of one's identity with Brahman. He illustrates this through narratives and metaphors that highlight the transformative power of love and devotion in the spiritual journey.

Tilak, in Gita Rahasya, focuses on Karma Yoga (the yoga of selfless action) as the primary means of realizing the self and fulfilling one's duty in society. He interprets Krishna's teachings to Arjuna as a call to action in the face of adversity, advocating the performance of righteous deeds (Dharma) without attachment to personal gain or recognition. For Tilak, self-realization is intertwined with social responsibility and the collective struggle for justice and freedom.

Comparative Analysis of Dnyaneshwari and Gita Rahasya on Karma Yoga

The concept of Karma Yoga, as explained in the Bhagavad Gita, emphasizes the path of selfless action performed without attachment to the results. It is a fundamental aspect of Hindu philosophy that guides individuals towards spiritual growth and liberation. Lokmanya Tilak through his Gita Rahasya and Sant Dnyaneshwar through his Dnyaneshwari, offer distinct interpretations of Karma Yoga, reflecting their unique philosophical perspectives and socio-cultural contexts.

Sant Dnyaneshwar provided a philosophical interpretation of Karma Yoga in his commentary. Dnyaneshwar interprets Karma Yoga as performing one's duties (svadharma) as an offering to God (Ishwara). He emphasizes a monist (Advaita) approach, where Karma Yoga is intertwined with the realization of the oneness of the self (Atman) and the ultimate reality (Brahman). For Dnyaneshwar, Karma Yoga is a path to spiritual enlightenment and liberation through understanding the unity of all existence. Dnyaneshwar's view on Karma Yoga is deeply rooted in the Bhakti tradition and emphasizes the integration of devotion with selfless action. He emphasizes that actions should be performed without attachment to their fruits, focusing instead on dedicating all actions to the divine. This attitude transforms mundane actions into acts of worship, purifying the mind and fostering spiritual growth. According to Dnyaneshwar, practicing Karma Yoga requires cultivating detachment (vairagya) towards the outcomes of actions. By relinquishing desires and expectations, individuals can maintain equanimity in success and failure, thereby transcending the dualities of joy and sorrow associated with worldly actions. Dnyaneshwar integrates Karma Yoga seamlessly with Bhakti Yoga, the path of loving devotion. He emphasizes that true Karma Yoga arises from a heart filled with devotion (Bhakti), where actions are performed with humility and a sense of duty towards God. For Dnyaneshwar, devotion enhances the purity of intentions behind actions, leading to spiritual elevation and union with the divine.

Lokmanya Bal Gangadhar Tilak offered a distinct interpretation of Karma Yoga in his work, Gita Rahasya. Tilak approaches Karma Yoga from a more pragmatic and practical perspective, focusing on duty and righteousness within the context of everyday life. His interpretation is influenced by the concept of Dharma and is more oriented towards practical action and societal responsibilities. His interpretation was deeply influenced by the socio-political context of colonial India and aimed to inspire patriotism and social reform through the teachings of the Gita. Tilak interpreted Karma Yoga primarily in the context of duty (dharma) towards society and nation. He emphasized that individuals should perform their prescribed duties selflessly, without attachment to personal gain, as a means to contribute to the welfare and upliftment of society. For Tilak, Karma Yoga was not just a spiritual practice but a call to action for national regeneration and social justice. Tilak viewed Karma Yoga as a transformative force that not only purifies the mind but also empowers individuals to strive toward personal and collective liberation. He interpreted Krishna's teachings in the Gita to emphasize the importance of righteous action (dharma) in upholding societal order and justice, thereby contributing to the greater good. Unlike Dnyaneshwar's focus on devotion and spiritual liberation, Tilak's interpretation of Karma Yoga emphasized its practical application in societal governance and reform. He sought to mobilize the masses through the teachings of the Gita, advocating for social and political engagement as a form of spiritual duty and service.

Dnyaneshwar emphasized Karma Yoga as a path integrated with Bhakti Yoga, focusing on devotion and surrender to God through selfless action. Tilak emphasized Karma Yoga as a duty towards society and nation, advocating for social and political engagement as a means to spiritual and national fulfilment.

Dnyaneshwar sees Karma Yoga as a means to attain spiritual wisdom and liberation (Moksha) by transcending the material world and realizing the unity of the self with the divine. Tilak views Karma Yoga as a means to fulfil one's duties and responsibilities in society while maintaining a sense of detachment. For Tilak, the practice of Karma Yoga is more about righteous action and selfless service in the context of one's role in society.

Dnyaneshwar rooted his interpretation in the medieval Bhakti tradition of Maharashtra, emphasizing personal devotion and surrender to divine will. Tilak influenced by the colonial socio-political context of India, framed his interpretation to inspire nationalistic fervour and social reform through Karma Yoga.

Dnyaneshwar viewed liberation (moksha) as the ultimate goal of Karma Yoga, attainable through devotion and selfless action performed as an offering to God. Tilak viewed liberation in terms of national and social liberation, advocating for freedom from colonial rule and societal injustices through righteous action and national service.

It can be concluded that Sant Dnyaneshwar and Lokmanya Tilak offered nuanced interpretations of Karma Yoga, reflecting their unique philosophical perspectives and socio-cultural contexts. They both strongly held on to the principle of selfless action as an essential element of Karma Yoga. Dnyaneshwar integrated Karma Yoga with Bhakti Yoga, emphasizing devotion and surrender to God through selfless action. Tilak, on the other hand, emphasized Karma Yoga as a duty towards society and nation, advocating for social and political engagement as a means to spiritual and national fulfilment. Both interpretations highlight the timeless relevance and depth of the Bhagavad Gita's teachings on Karma Yoga, offering insights into its application in personal, social, and spiritual domains across different historical and cultural contexts.

Comparative analysis of Dnyaneshwari and Gita Rahasya on Bhakti Yoga

Bhakti Yoga, the path of loving devotion to the divine, is a central theme in the Bhagavad Gita, revered as one of the primary paths to spiritual realization and liberation. Sant Dnyaneshwar and Lokmanya Tilak, both, influential figures in Indian history, offered distinct interpretations of Bhakti Yoga, reflecting their contextual perspectives. I shall attempt to explore their interpretations of Bhakti Yoga and provide a comparative analysis of their viewpoints, drawing insights from their respective works and contributions.

Dnyaneshwar emphasizes that Bhakti (devotion) is the essence of connecting with the divine. He interprets Krishna's teachings in the Gita as emphasizing the significance of surrendering oneself completely to God and cultivating a loving relationship with the divine. According to Dnyaneshwar, true knowledge (jnana) arises from a heart filled with devotion rather than from mere intellectual understanding. Central to Dnyaneshwari is the concept of surrender (prapatti), where the seeker relinquishes personal desires and ego to the divine will (Ishwara prapatti). He portrays Lord Krishna as the Supreme Being who incarnates to guide humanity towards spiritual liberation through unwavering devotion and surrender. While emphasizing Bhakti Yoga, Dnyaneshwar also integrates other paths to spiritual realization, including Karma Yoga (the path of selfless action) and Jnana Yoga (the path of knowledge). He presents an integrated approach to spiritual practice, where devotion, selfless action, and self-inquiry converge to lead the seeker towards union with the divine.

Tilak interpreted Bhakti Yoga primarily in the context of national duty (dharma) and devotion to the nation. He emphasized that individuals should cultivate a deep love and commitment (Bhakti) towards their country and society, viewing devotion as a unifying force that inspires selfless service and sacrifice for the nation. Unlike Dnyaneshwar's focus on personal devotion and surrender to God, Tilak's interpretation of Bhakti Yoga emphasized its role in fostering nationalistic fervour and social reform. He viewed Bhakti as a transformative force that not only uplifts individuals spiritually but also mobilizes them towards collective action for national regeneration and social justice. Tilak's interpretation of Bhakti Yoga emphasized its practical application in societal governance and reform. He sought to awaken the masses through the teachings of the Gita, advocating for social and political engagement as a form of spiritual duty and service towards the nation.

Dnyaneshwar emphasized Bhakti Yoga as the path of loving devotion to God, viewing devotion as essential for spiritual realization and union with the divine. Tilak emphasized Bhakti Yoga as devotion to the nation and society, advocating for national duty and social reform as expressions of devotion and service.

Dnyaneshwar rooted his interpretation in the medieval Bhakti tradition of Maharashtra, focusing on personal surrender and devotion to divine grace. Tilak influenced by the colonial socio-political context of India, framed his interpretation to inspire nationalistic fervour and social reform through Bhakti Yoga.

Dnyaneshwar viewed Bhakti Yoga as a path to spiritual liberation (moksha), emphasizing the transformation of the individual through loving devotion and surrender. Tilak viewed Bhakti Yoga as a means to national and social fulfilment, advocating for spiritual and social regeneration through devotion and selfless service.

Sant Dnyaneshwar and Lokmanya Tilak offered distinctive interpretations of Bhakti Yoga, reflecting their unique philosophical perspectives and socio-cultural contexts. Dnyaneshwar emphasized Bhakti Yoga as the path of loving devotion to God, highlighting surrender and divine grace as essential elements of spiritual practice. In contrast, Tilak interpreted Bhakti Yoga in the context of national duty and devotion to the nation, advocating for social and political engagement as expressions of devotion and service. Both, Dnyaneshwar, and Tilak converged on a view that Bhakti Yoga is a path towards spiritual, moral, and societal well-being, tailored to their respective historical and cultural contexts.

Comparative analysis of Dnyaneshwari and Gita Rahasya on Jnana Yoga

Jnana Yoga, the path of knowledge and wisdom, occupies a significant place in the teachings of the Bhagavad Gita, offering seekers a pathway to spiritual enlightenment through self-inquiry and understanding of the true nature of existence. Sant Dnyaneshwar and Lokmanya Tilak, provided distinct interpretations of Jnana Yoga, reflecting their unique philosophical perspectives and socio-cultural contexts.

Sant Dnyaneshwar's interpretation of Jnana Yoga is deeply rooted in the Advaita Vedanta tradition and emphasizes the path of knowledge as a means to attain spiritual liberation. Dnyaneshwar explains that Jnana Yoga involves the pursuit of knowledge of the true Self (Atman). He interprets Krishna's teachings in the Gita to emphasize self-inquiry and introspection as essential for realizing one's true nature beyond the limitations of the ego and body. According to Dnyaneshwar, true knowledge (jnana) arises from direct experience and realization of the Self. Central to Dnyaneshwari is the concept of discrimination (viveka) between the eternal and the transient, and detachment (vairagya) from worldly attachments. He emphasizes that Jnana Yoga requires discernment to distinguish between the impermanent aspects of existence (nama-rupa) and the eternal essence (Brahman), leading to liberation from the cycle of birth and death. While emphasizing Jnana Yoga, Dnyaneshwar also integrates Bhakti Yoga (the path of devotion) into his commentary. He views devotion as essential in harmonizing intellect with emotion, thereby facilitating a comprehensive approach to spiritual realization. For Dnyaneshwar, Jnana Yoga and Bhakti Yoga converge in realizing the non-dual nature of existence and attaining union with the divine.

Lokmanya Bal Gangadhar Tilak provided a distinctive interpretation of Jnana Yoga in his work "Gita Rahasya". He interpreted Jnana Yoga primarily as the path of intellectual inquiry and knowledge (jnana). He emphasized the importance of philosophical discernment and understanding the true nature of existence as described in the teachings of Krishna in the Bhagavad Gita. According to Tilak, Jnana Yoga leads to the realization of the eternal Self (Atman) and liberation from ignorance (avidya). Unlike Dnyaneshwar's focus on personal realization and spiritual liberation, Tilak's interpretation of Jnana Yoga emphasized its role in fostering intellectual clarity and social reform. He viewed Jnana Yoga as empowering individuals with the knowledge to discern truth from falsehood and to engage in social and political activism for national regeneration and justice. Tilak's interpretation of Jnana Yoga emphasized its practical application in societal governance and reform. He sought to awaken the masses through the teachings of the Gita, advocating for the cultivation of wisdom and knowledge as a means to uplift society and combat oppression.

Dnyaneshwar emphasized Jnana Yoga as the path of self-realization through knowledge of the true Self (Atman), integrating Bhakti Yoga for holistic spiritual growth. Tilak emphasized Jnana Yoga as intellectual inquiry and knowledge, highlighting its role in social reform and national regeneration through philosophical discernment.

Dnyaneshwar rooted his interpretation in Advaita Vedanta and the Bhakti tradition of Maharashtra, focusing on personal liberation and union with the divine. Tilak influenced by the colonial socio-political context of India, framed his interpretation to inspire nationalistic fervour and social reform through intellectual enlightenment.

Dnyaneshwar viewed liberation (moksha) as the ultimate goal of Jnana Yoga, attainable through self-realization and realization of the eternal Self. Tilak viewed liberation in terms of social and national liberation, advocating for freedom from ignorance and oppression through philosophical inquiry and social reform.

To sum it up, Dnyaneshwar emphasized Jnana Yoga as the path of self-realization and union with the divine, integrating Bhakti Yoga for holistic spiritual growth. Tilak, on the other hand, interpreted Jnana Yoga primarily as intellectual inquiry and knowledge, emphasizing its role in fostering social reform and national regeneration through philosophical discernment and activism.

Philosophical dimensions of literature evolve with time

The Gita Rahasya and Dnyaneshwari stand as compelling testimonies to how the philosophical dimensions of literature evolve with the passage of time. These texts, rooted in ancient wisdom and spiritual insight, have continuously adapted to resonate with shifting societal paradigms and philosophical inquiries. Originally penned to explain profound truths about existence, morality, and the human condition, they have transcended their historical contexts to offer perennial guidance and inspiration across centuries. In examining these scriptures, we witness their ability to remain relevant by addressing contemporary philosophical concerns and socio-political challenges. They provide a framework for understanding ethical dilemmas, governance principles, and the pursuit of spiritual enlightenment amidst changing landscapes. The Gita Rahasya and Dnyaneshwari, through their reinterpretations and commentaries over time, exemplify literature's dynamic nature and its capacity to engage with new generations in meaningful dialogue.

As they continue to provoke introspection and debate, these texts underscore literature's role as a timeless repository of philosophical exploration, enriching our understanding of the world and our place within it. Their enduring relevance lies in their ability to transcend the limitations of their origins, offering insights that resonate with humanity's perennial quest for meaning and truth in an ever-changing world. Thus, they illuminate how literature's philosophical dimensions adapt and endure, shaping our intellectual discourse and spiritual inquiries across the ages.

Conclusion

Comparative analysis of philosophical perspectives between Dnyaneshwari and Gita Rahasya spans a rich repository of ideas, interpretations, and implications drawn from these seminal commentaries on the Bhagavad Gita. It involves examining their respective philosophical frameworks, theological interpretations, and socio-cultural contexts to distil the essence of their contributions to Indian thought. Sant Dnyaneshwar, through his Dnyaneshwari, illuminates the path of devotion (Bhakti) and philosophy of monism (Advaita Vedanta) as pathways to self-realization and spiritual liberation. His commentary, rooted in the Nath tradition and steeped in the linguistic and literary richness of Marathi, transcends mere scholarly discourse to resonate deeply with the hearts and minds of his audience. Dnyaneshwar's interpretation of the Bhagavad Gita emphasizes the unity of the individual soul (Jivatma) with the universal soul (Paramatma), advocating an integrated approach to spirituality that integrates inner transformation with ethical living. His use of poetic language, metaphors, and allegories not only reveals the Gita's teachings but also invites readers into a transformative journey of self-discovery and divine communion.

In contrast, Bal Gangadhar Tilak's Gita Rahasya emerges as a bold reinterpretation of the Gita's teachings within the socio-political landscape of colonial India. Tilak, a nationalist leader, and intellectual powerhouse, frames his commentary through the lens of Karma Yoga and the concept of selfless action (Nishkama Karma), advocating for a moral and ethical framework that aligns individual duty (Svadharma) with the larger cause of national liberation. His interpretation of the Gita's philosophical underpinnings emphasizes on the imperative of social justice, collective responsibility, and moral courage in the face of adversity. Through rigorous scholarship and logical reasoning, Tilak presents Krishna's dialogue with Arjuna as a call to action, inspiring a generation of Indians to rise against colonial oppression and uphold the ideals of freedom, justice, and self-determination.

The comparative analysis of Dnyaneshwari and Gita Rahasya reveals complementary yet distinct philosophical perspectives on fundamental concepts such as the nature of the self (Atman), the paths to spiritual realization, and the ethical foundations of human existence. Dnyaneshwar's emphasis on Bhakti and Advaita Vedanta offers a deeply personal and experiential approach to understanding the self as inherently divine and united with the cosmos. His commentary fosters a sense of spiritual unity and harmony, encouraging individuals to transcend egoic limitations and embrace their innate divinity through devotion and self-surrender. Conversely, Tilak's nationalist interpretation of the Gita stresses on the dynamic interplay between individual agency and social responsibility in shaping historical destinies. His philosophical framework, grounded in practical ethics and socio-political activism, challenges readers to confront societal injustices and uphold the principles of righteousness and moral integrity. Tilak's Gita Rahasya not only serves as a scholarly commentary but also as a manifesto for political awakening and national resurgence, harnessing the ethical teachings of the Gita to inspire collective action and transformative change. To conclude, the comparative analysis of Dnyaneshwari and Gita Rahasya accentuates their enduring relevance and transformative impact on Indian philosophy, spirituality, and socio-political discourse. Together, these commentaries exemplify the richness and diversity of Indian intellectual traditions, offering timeless insights into the human quest for meaning, purpose, and ethical conduct in an ever-changing world.

Author's Notes:

Authorship of Bhagavad Gita, Dnyaneshwari, and Gita Rahasya

Traditional belief in Indian history attributes authorship of Bhagavad Gita to Veda Vyasa, alone. However, a set of scholars also believe that Vyasa is a natural attribution or a symbolic author of the Gita because he is also credited as a compiler of Vedas and Puranas which texts are dated from different time periods. Dr. Gajanan Khair proposes a theory that Bhagavad Gita was rather compiled by three distinct authors over a period of time with each contributing different philosophical perspectives to the text. In his book, 'Quest for the Original Gita' he argues that stylistic and thematic shifts within the Gita point to multiple authorship. Indologist Arthur Basham takes a similar view in his book "The origins and development of Classical Hinduism" to state that there were at least two more hands that added to the 'original Bhagavad Gita'. He arrives at this conclusion based on the discontinuous intermixing of philosophical verses with theistic or passionately theistic verses. Alexus McLeod, a scholar of Philosophy and Asian Studies suggests that it is "impossible to link the Bhagavad Gita to a single author:" While making this Argument in his book 'Understanding Asian Philosophy' McLeod suggests that Bhagavad Gita, which is part of a larger epic Mahabharata, reflects a synthesis of diverse philosophical traditions and cultural influences that evolved over centuries. McLeod's assertion emphasizes the Gita's role as a dynamic philosophical dialogue rather than a static work of a singular genius.

Dnyaneshwari and Gita Rahasya and the philosophy contained in them can be singularly attributed to their authors - Sant Dnyaneshwar and Lokmanya Tilak. The years of distilled wisdom embedded in the Gita, accumulated over generations, was masterfully encapsulated by Dnyaneshwar and Tilak, who crafted a unidimensional narrative that resonated profoundly with the unique contexts of their respective eras.

II Study Sources on Dnyaneshwari

Primary study and understanding of Dnyaneshwari was undertaken by referring to "Shree Dnyanehswari by Mamasaheb Dandekar" and "Sarth Dnyaneshwari by Shri Nana Maharaj Sakhre" (both in Marathi). "Shrimad Gita Rahasya" in Marathi and English by Lokmanya Tilak (including english translation by B S Sukhtankar) was the primary source for the study of Gita Rahasya.

References

"Comparative Literature: A Very Short Introduction" by Ben Hutchinson. This book is an insightful guide that helps understand the methodology and significance of comparative analysis in literature. It offers frameworks and strategies for undertaking a comparative study of literary works.

Other references

Dr. Gajanan Shripat Khair (1969), Quest for the Original Gita

Alexus McLeod (2014), Understanding Asian Philosophy

Arthur Llewellyn Basham (1991). The Origins and Development of Classical Hinduism

Chapter 4

Literary Analysis

Paths to Enlightenment – comparative literary themes in Dnyaneshwari and Gita Rahasya

Dnyaneshwari – Literary analysis

I

"Dnyaneshwari" was composed by Sant Dnyaneshwar in the Marathi language around 1290 CE. Sant Dnyaneshwar hailed from a lineage of Nath yogis and was initiated into spiritual practices from an immature age. His commentary on the Bhagavad Gita is notable for being one of the earliest translations into a regional Indian language, making the Gita's teachings accessible to the masses who were not proficient in Sanskrit. "Dnyaneshwari" consists of 9,929 verses composed in ovi meter, a traditional Marathi verse form. The commentary follows the format of an ongoing dialogue between Sant Dnyaneshwar and his disciple, Sacchidananda, who represents the seeker of knowledge. This format allows for a dynamic exploration of the Gita's verses, where each chapter of the Gita is sequentially explained and expanded upon by Sant Dnyaneshwar.

Sant Dnyaneshwar's language in "Dnyaneshwari" is poetic, and rich in metaphor, allegory, and simile. His verses evoke deep emotional and spiritual resonance, capturing the essence of the Gita's teachings in lyrical prose. The use of Marathi and at times the colloquial marathi phrases enhances accessibility, making complex philosophical concepts understandable to a wider audience. The narrative technique of "Dnyaneshwari" blends exposition with dialogues and discourses. Sant Dnyaneshwar often uses anecdotes, stories from Hindu mythology, and everyday experiences to illustrate abstract philosophical concepts. This narrative approach not only interprets the Gita's teachings but also engages the reader in a profound spiritual inquiry. Sant Dnyaneshwar integrates Advaita Vedanta (monist philosophy) with Bhakti (devotional) elements in his commentary. He emphasizes the unity of the individual soul (Jivatma) with the universal soul (Paramatma), presenting a vision of spiritual realization through love, devotion, and self-surrender. His interpretation reconciles the apparent dualities of existence, advocating for a holistic understanding of the self and its relationship to the divine.

II

Sant Dnyaneshwar explores the nature of the self (Atman) as eternal, immutable, and inherently divine. He explains how the individual soul, though seemingly separate, is fundamentally one with the cosmic consciousness (Brahman). His commentary fosters a deep introspective inquiry into the nature of identity, existence, and ultimate reality. "Dnyaneshwari" delineates various paths to spiritual liberation (Moksha), emphasizing the efficacy of devotion (Bhakti), selfless action (Karma Yoga), and knowledge (Jnana) in attaining union with the divine. Sant Dnyaneshwar's comprehensive approach integrates these paths, offering practical guidance for seekers on their spiritual journey. The commentary addresses ethical dilemmas and moral conduct, advocating for righteousness (Dharma) and compassion in thought, word, and deed. Sant Dnyaneshwar's teachings promote social harmony, universal love, and the inherent unity of all beings, transcending caste, and societal divisions. "Dnyaneshwari" has left an indelible mark on Marathi literature, Hindu philosophy, and spiritual discourse. Its profound insights into the Bhagavad Gita's teachings continue to inspire generations of readers, scholars, and spiritual seekers. Sant Dnyaneshwar's commentary remains relevant for its timeless wisdom, spiritual depth, and inclusive vision of humanity's quest for self-realization and divine communion.

"Dnyaneshwari" by Sant Dnyaneshwar stands as a masterpiece of Marathi literature and philosophical exposition. Through its poetic language, narrative richness, and profound insights, the commentary illuminates the Bhagavad Gita's teachings on the nature of the self, pathways to liberation, and ethical conduct. Sant Dnyaneshwar's synthesis of Advaita Vedanta and Bhakti philosophy offers a holistic understanding of spirituality, emphasizing the unity of the individual soul with the universal soul. "Dnyaneshwari" continues to inspire and guide spiritual seekers on their quest for self-realization and divine wisdom, embodying the timeless relevance of its teachings in contemporary times.

Gita Rahasya – literary analysis

I

Bal Gangadhar Tilak wrote "Gita Rahasya" in 1915 while imprisoned by the British colonial authorities. His commentary on the Bhagavad Gita was intended to inspire and mobilize Indians in their fight against colonial oppression. Tilak's interpretation combines deep philosophical insights with practical socio-political implications, making "Gita Rahasya" a unique blend of spiritual discourse and nationalist ideology. "Gita Rahasya" consists of two parts: the philosophical exposition (titled "Karma Yoga Shastra") and the socio-political commentary (titled "Bhakti Yoga Shastra"). Tilak diligently analyses each verse of the Bhagavad Gita across nineteen chapters, offering interpretations that emphasize Gita's teachings on karma yoga (the yoga of action), selfless duty, and the ethical imperatives of righteousness and justice. His commentary is structured and systematic, reflecting Tilak's background as a legal scholar and political activist.

Unlike traditional Sanskrit commentaries, "Gita Rahasya" is written in clear and accessible Marathi prose. Tilak's style is analytical and logical, characterized by systematic argumentation and rigorous scholarly analysis. He employs Sanskrit terminology judiciously, ensuring that his interpretations are rooted in the original text while making them understandable to a wider audience. Tilak uses rhetorical devices such as analogies, historical references, and comparative analysis to clarify the Gita's teachings. His use of examples from Indian history and mythology serves to illustrate philosophical concepts and reinforce his nationalist interpretation of the text. "Gita Rahasya" inquiries into the philosophical underpinnings of Gita's teachings, particularly focusing on the nature of the self (Atman), the concept of dharma (righteous duty), and the paths to spiritual realization.

Tilak's commentary emphasizes the importance of karma yoga as a means of achieving personal growth, social harmony, and national resurgence.

II

Central to "Gita Rahasya" is Tilak's interpretation of the Gita's teachings on duty (dharma) and action (karma). He argues that individuals have a moral obligation to perform their duties selflessly, without attachment to personal gain or recognition. Tilak's nationalist perspective frames these teachings within the context of India's struggle for independence, encouraging readers to uphold principles of righteousness and justice in the face of colonial oppression. Tilak emphasizes the ethical imperatives of the Gita, advocating for a moral framework based on truth, integrity, and social responsibility. His commentary underlines the importance of ethical conduct in personal life and governance, drawing parallels between the teachings of the Gita and contemporary socio-political challenges. While Tilak's focus is primarily on karma yoga and socio-political activism, "Gita Rahasya" also touches upon themes of spiritual liberation (moksha) and the realization of the self (Atman). He interprets Krishna's dialogue with Arjuna as a transformative journey towards self-awareness and divine consciousness, highlighting Gita's teachings on the eternal nature of the soul and its relationship to the material world. "Gita Rahasya" has had a profound impact on Indian intellectual and political thought. Tilak's nationalist interpretation of the Bhagavad Gita inspired a generation of freedom fighters and activists during India's struggle for independence. His commentary continues to be studied for its insights into karma yoga, ethical governance, and the enduring relevance of ancient Indian wisdom in contemporary times.

"Gita Rahasya" by Bal Gangadhar Tilak stands as a monumental work of literary and philosophical significance. Through his analytical prose and nationalist fervour, Tilak offers a compelling reinterpretation of the Bhagavad Gita's teachings, emphasizing the principles of karma yoga, ethical duty, and social justice. His commentary not only reveals the timeless wisdom of the Gita but also serves as a manifesto for moral courage, national pride, and spiritual awakening. "Gita Rahasya" continues to resonate with readers for its intellectual rigor, socio-political relevance, and profound insights into the nature of human existence and ethical conduct.

Linguistic and Stylistic analysis

The linguistic and stylistic nuances of Dnyaneshwari and Gita Rahasya further enrich their philosophical discourses. Dnyaneshwar's use of the regional language Marathi, infused with poetic beauty and cultural resonance, facilitates a deep emotional and intellectual engagement with the Gita's teachings, making spirituality accessible to a diverse audience. In contrast, Tilak's Sanskrit prose and analytical approach appeal to scholars and activists alike, providing a structured framework for interpreting Gita's ethical imperatives within the context of colonial subjugation and national resurgence.

Language and dialectal expression

I

Dnyaneshwari is written in Marathi, making the teachings of the Gita accessible to the common people of Maharashtra. Sant Dnyaneshwar's use of poetic language, metaphors, and colloquial expressions enriches the commentary, enhancing its emotional and philosophical depth. The dialectal style of Dnyaneshwari facilitates a direct and intimate engagement with the spiritual teachings of the Gita, appealing to both scholarly audiences and the general populace. Dnyaneshwari exemplifies the transformative power of language and dialectal expression in conveying spiritual wisdom and philosophical insight. One of the most significant aspects of "Dnyaneshwari" is its use of Marathi and its colloquial expressions. Sant Dnyaneshwar deliberately chose Marathi, the language of the common people, to convey the teachings of the Gita. This decision democratized spiritual knowledge, allowing individuals from diverse backgrounds and castes to engage directly with the scripture without the mediation of Sanskrit scholars. Sant Dnyaneshwar's language in "Dnyaneshwari" is poetic and lyrical, employing various literary devices such as similes, metaphors, and allegories. His verses are imbued with emotive depth and spiritual resonance, creating a profound impact on the reader's mind and heart. Through poetic expression, he conveys complex philosophical ideas in a manner that is both intellectually stimulating and emotionally evocative. "Dnyaneshwari" follows a narrative format where Sant Dnyaneshwar engages in a dialogue with his disciple, Sachchidananda. This dialogic structure not only facilitates a deeper exploration of Gita's verses but also allows for the integration of personal insights, anecdotes, and everyday examples to clarify abstract concepts. The narrative technique enhances readability and comprehension, transforming philosophical discourse into a relatable and transformative experience for the reader. Sant Dnyaneshwar's use of Marathi is rooted in the cultural context of Maharashtra. This cultural resonance strengthens the connection between the text and its readers, fostering a deeper engagement with the spiritual teachings imparted in "Dnyaneshwari." The literary richness of "Dnyaneshwari" reflects Sant Dnyaneshwar's commitment to inclusivity and universality in spiritual discourse. By using Marathi, he transcends linguistic barriers and invites individuals from all walks of life to partake in the transformative wisdom of the Gita. This inclusive approach underlines the democratic spirit of Sant Dnyaneshwar's teachings, affirming the accessibility of spiritual knowledge irrespective of social status or educational background.

By employing metaphors, colloquialisms, idioms, and proverbs familiar to his audience, Dnyaneshwar creates a sense of cultural intimacy and authenticity. Metaphors in Dnyaneshwari serve to illustrate abstract concepts and make them more tangible for the reader. Dnyaneshwar's metaphors often draw upon natural imagery, everyday life, and cultural symbols to explain the deeper meanings of the Gita's verses. At a juncture Dnyaneshwar compares the Bhagavad Gita to a mango tree laden with ripe fruits, bending low under its weight. This metaphor symbolizes the abundance of spiritual knowledge contained within the scripture and the profound impact it has on those who dive deep into its teachings. Dnyaneshwar employs the metaphor of the ocean to depict the unshakable calm and detachment of a wise person amidst worldly desires. Just as the ocean remains undisturbed by the rivers flowing into it, so do the sages remain unmoved by the desires that enter their mind. Colloquialisms in Dnyaneshwari contribute to its accessibility and relatability, creating a conversational tone that engages the reader directly. Throughout Dnyaneshwari, Dnyaneshwar addresses Arjuna in colloquial Marathi, fostering a personal and intimate dialogue between the reader and the characters of the Gita. This colloquialism makes the philosophical discourse more immediate and relevant to the reader's spiritual journey. Dnyaneshwari often adopts a conversational style where Dnyaneshwar speaks directly to his disciple, Sachchidananda. This approach not only explains the Gita's verses but also encourages a deeper reflection on their practical application in everyday life. Dnyaneshwar incorporates Marathi idioms and proverbs to emphasize moral teachings, cultural values, and ethical principles found in the Bhagavad Gita. Dnyaneshwari includes idiomatic expressions that resonate with the cultural context of Maharashtra, such as references to farming, village life, professions, and familial relationships. These idioms enrich the narrative with cultural authenticity and connect the spiritual teachings of the Gita to everyday experiences. Firstly, these literary devices make the profound philosophical concepts of the Bhagavad Gita accessible and understandable to a wide audience, transcending linguistic and cultural barriers. Secondly, they enrich the text with emotional depth, cultural resonance, and poetic imagery, enhancing the reader's engagement and appreciation of the spiritual teachings. Lastly, these devices underscore Dnyaneshwar's role as a poet-saint who not only interpreted the Gita's verses but also infused them with the vibrant mosaic of Marathi language and culture. Dnyaneshwar's skilful use of metaphors, colloquialisms, idioms, and proverbs in Dnyaneshwari demonstrates his mastery as a poet, philosopher, and spiritual guide. Through these literary devices, he invites readers on a transformative journey of self-discovery and spiritual enlightenment, making Dnyaneshwari a timeless and revered text in Marathi literature and Hindu philosophy.

In his book Dnyaneshwaritil Jeev Srishti (*Life forms in Dnyaneshwari*), Dr. Thatte emphasizes the literary references to life forms in the Dnyaneshwari to illustrate the interconnectedness of all existence as envisioned by Sant Dnyaneshwar. He argues that Dnyaneshwar's vivid imagery and analogies involving various life forms serve not only to enrich the text's philosophical discourse but also to ground abstract spiritual concepts in the tangible realities of life. By drawing parallels between human experiences and the broader spectrum of life from plants to animals, Dnyaneshwar highlights the fundamental unity of all beings, inviting readers to contemplate their place within this interconnected web. Dr. Thatte further asserts that these references encourage a holistic understanding of existence, urging readers to recognize the sanctity of all life and fostering a sense of empathy and responsibility toward the natural world. This emphasis on life forms reinforces the ethical and moral dimensions of Dnyaneshwar's teachings, making them relevant across generations and prompting deeper reflection on the relationship between spirituality and the environment.

II

Gita Rahasya, on the other hand, is written in Sanskrit prose, reflecting Tilak's background in classical scholarship and legal studies. Tilak's writing is characterized by its clarity, precision, and systematic exposition of philosophical concepts. His use of Sanskrit terminology and analytical approach further clarifies his intent to present a scholarly interpretation of the Gita's teachings, informed by his socio-political context and nationalist ideology.

"Gita Rahasya" is primarily written in Marathi prose, with Sanskrit verses from the Bhagavad Gita interspersed throughout the text. Tilak's use of Marathi makes the commentary accessible to a wider audience, including those who may not be fluent in Sanskrit but are familiar with the regional language of Maharashtra. Tilak's language in "Gita Rahasya" is characterized by its logical and analytical approach. As a trained lawyer and scholar, Tilak presents his arguments systematically, drawing upon Sanskrit terminology and philosophical concepts to expound upon the Gita's verses. His prose is clear and structured, reflecting his background in legal reasoning and intellectual discourse. Tilak employs rhetorical devices such as analogies, historical references, and comparative analysis to reveal the Gita's teachings. Throughout "Gita Rahasya," Tilak quotes extensively from the Bhagavad Gita itself, as well as from other Hindu scriptures and philosophical texts. He uses these quotations to support his interpretations and to establish a scholarly foundation for his commentary. Quoting authoritative texts enhances Tilak's credibility as a commentator and strengthens the philosophical underpinnings of his arguments. It also invites readers to engage directly with the original sources, fostering a deeper understanding of the Gita's teachings. Tilak poses rhetorical questions to provoke thought and introspection in his readers. For instance, he asks whether the pursuit of duty (dharma) should be compromised in the face of adversity or injustice. Rhetorical questions encourage readers to contemplate ethical dilemmas and moral choices presented in the Gita. They stimulate critical thinking and encourage a deeper engagement with Tilak's interpretations of karma yoga and righteous action. Tilak uses emotive language to stir nationalist sentiment and moral conviction among his readers. He appeals to their sense of duty and patriotism, urging them to emulate Arjuna's resolve and courage in the face of oppression. Emotive language and appeals to emotion mobilize readers emotionally and intellectually, aligning them with Tilak's vision of social reform and national resurgence. This rhetorical strategy galvanizes support for Tilak's interpretation of the Gita as a call to action against injustice and colonial rule. Tilak employs logical reasoning and structured argumentation to systematically analyze each verse of the Bhagavad Gita. He presents his interpretations in a clear, coherent manner, using logic to substantiate his views on karma yoga, selfless action, and spiritual liberation. Logical argumentation enhances the persuasive power of Tilak's commentary, appealing to readers' intellect and rationality. It establishes a logical framework for understanding Gita's philosophical teachings and their application to individual conduct and societal ethics. These devices not only enhance the clarity and persuasiveness of Tilak's commentary but also evoke a sense of cultural pride, moral responsibility, and national unity among his readers. By employing these rhetorical strategies, Tilak transforms philosophical discourse into a compelling call to action, advocating for ethical conduct, social justice, and spiritual enlightenment through the timeless wisdom of the Gita.

While "Gita Rahasya" is rooted in Sanskrit philosophy, Tilak imbues his commentary with regional expressions that resonate with the nationalist sentiment of his time. He invokes cultural symbols, historical events, and myths to illustrate the Gita's message of duty, righteousness, and moral courage in the face of oppression. Tilak draws upon Marathi cultural references, proverbs, and idioms to emphasize the practical application of the Gita's teachings in everyday life. This cultural grounding serves to connect the philosophical discourse with the lived experiences of his readers, thereby enhancing its relevance and impact.

Poetic and Literary Techniques

I

Dnyaneshwari employs a blend of narrative, dialogue, and exposition to explain the Gita's teachings. Sant Dnyaneshwar integrates metaphysical insights with devotional fervour, employing poetic devices such as simile, allegory, and symbolism to convey profound spiritual truths. His commentary unfolds through a series of discourses (Pravachans) that engage the reader in a dialogue with the divine wisdom of the Gita.

Dnyaneshwar uses Similes in Dnyaneshwari to draw parallels between physical phenomena and spiritual realities, thereby elucidating complex concepts for the reader. In several instances, Dnyaneshwar uses the simile of the ocean to illustrate the boundless and undisturbed nature of the enlightened soul (jivanmukta). Just as the ocean remains unaffected by the rivers that flow into it, so does the sage remain unaffected by the desires that arise in the mind. At times, Dnyaneshwar compares the illuminating nature of the Supreme Brahman to a lamp that lights up everything around it. This simile highlights the role of divine consciousness in dispelling ignorance and revealing the true nature of reality to the seeker. Allegories in Dnyaneshwari serve to convey deeper philosophical truths through symbolic narratives and storytelling. Dnyaneshwar uses the allegory of the chariot to depict the composition of the human body-mind complex. The chariot represents the physical body, the horses symbolize the senses, the reins signify the mind, and the charioteer represents the intellect.

This allegory reveals the dynamics of self-control and the mastery of the senses discussed in the Gita. Dnyaneshwar employs the allegory of the mango tree laden with ripe fruits to illustrate the significance of the Bhagavad Gita as the essence of the Vedas. Just as the mango tree bows down under the weight of its fruits, so is the Gita revered for its abundant spiritual wisdom and transformative teachings. Symbolism in Dnyaneshwari imbues objects, actions, and concepts with deeper meanings that resonate with spiritual and philosophical themes. Light symbolizes knowledge, wisdom, and spiritual illumination, while darkness represents ignorance, delusion, and material attachments. Dnyaneshwar frequently employs this symbolism to contrast the paths of righteousness (dharma) and ignorance (adharma) discussed in the Gita. Dnyaneshwar uses the symbolism of the lotus to depict the purity and detachment of the enlightened soul. Just as a lotus blooms untouched by the muddy waters it grows in, so does the sage remain unaffected by the worldly temptations and dualities of life. These poetic devices of simile, allegory, and symbolism in Dnyaneshwari, enhance its poetic impact and spiritual depth in several ways as they create a vivid visual imagery that engages the reader's imagination, evokes an emotional resonance to connect deeply with the spiritual principles, and also allow Dnyaneshwar to explore universal themes of human experience such as love and suffering. All these help bring abstract philosophical concepts to life. Purely from a linguistic standpoint, Dnyaneshwar can be seen as a scholar.

II

Central to the poetic structure of Dnyaneshwari is the use of the "Ovi" meter, a traditional Marathi verse form that highlights Dnyaneshwar's poetic genius and mastery of language. The following passage explores the significance of the Ovi meter in Dnyaneshwari and its contribution to Dnyaneshwar's enduring legacy as a poet-saint. The Ovi meter is a distinctive feature of Marathi poetry, characterized by its compact and lyrical form. Each Ovi consists of four lines (quatrains) with a fixed number of syllables and a specific rhythmic pattern. Traditionally, an Ovi contains eight syllables per line, resulting in a structured and melodious verse that is well-suited for oral recitation and musical adaptation.

The Ovi meter's rhythmic structure lends itself to a lyrical flow that enhances the musicality and memorability of Dnyaneshwari. This rhythmic cadence, combined with Dnyaneshwar's skilful use of language and imagery, creates a captivating poetic experience for the reader. Despite its concise form, the Ovi meter allows Dnyaneshwar to maintain clarity and coherence in his exposition of complex philosophical concepts. Each quatrain encapsulates a complete thought or idea, facilitating a systematic exploration of the Bhagavad Gita's teachings.

Dnyaneshwar's use of the Ovi meter demonstrates his innovative approach to poetic expression within the literary conventions of his time. He employs various poetic devices such as metaphors, similes, allegories, and symbolism to elucidate spiritual truths, enriching the Ovi meter with layers of meaning and depth. Dnyaneshwar integrates elements of Marathi culture, folklore, and religious symbolism into his verses, resonating deeply with the cultural identity and spiritual ethos of Maharashtra. His poetic genius lies in his ability to weave together philosophical discourse with cultural specificity, making Dnyaneshwari both timeless and culturally relevant. Dnyaneshwari's use of the Ovi meter has had a profound influence on Marathi literature and poetry, inspiring generations of poets and scholars. The Ovi meter continues to be revered for its aesthetic beauty and expressive versatility, embodying the enduring legacy of Dnyaneshwar as a pioneer of Marathi literary tradition. Through the rhythmic beauty and lyrical grace of the

Ovi meter, Dnyaneshwar eloquently conveys profound spiritual truths while maintaining narrative clarity and cultural resonance.

III

In contrast, Gita Rahasya adopts a more straightforward and analytical style, characterized by logical reasoning and systematic argumentation. Tilak's commentary is structured around a rigorous interpretation of the Gita's verses, supplemented by historical and cultural references to illustrate his nationalist interpretation of Karma Yoga and the concept of selfless duty. His prose is marked by its depth, clarity, and intellectual rigor, aiming to appeal to both scholars and political activists of his time.

Tilak's writing in "Gita Rahasya" is marked by clarity and precision in presenting complex philosophical ideas. He painstakingly analyses each verse of the Bhagavad Gita, unravelling its layers of meaning and relevance to human existence. Tilak's ability to interpret complex metaphysical concepts in a straightforward manner makes "Gita Rahasya" accessible to readers of varying backgrounds, from scholars to laypersons seeking spiritual enlightenment. His writing reflects a profound engagement with Hindu philosophy, drawing on classical commentaries and his interpretations to offer insights into the nature of the self, the universe, and the divine. As a scholar well-versed in Sanskrit and Hindu scriptures, Tilak employs a rigorous methodology in "Gita Rahasya." He cites original Sanskrit verses from the Bhagavad Gita and other scriptures, providing textual evidence to support his interpretations. Tilak's scholarly approach includes a comparative analysis of different commentaries and philosophical schools, offering a comprehensive view of the Gita's teachings and their implications. Tilak's language in "Gita Rahasya" is scholarly yet accessible, blending Sanskrit terminology with Marathi prose to convey complex ideas with clarity. His writing style is authoritative yet engaging, employing rhetorical devices such as analogies, historical references, and logical arguments to strengthen his interpretations. Tilak's prose is imbued with a sense of urgency and conviction, reflecting his commitment to social reform and national regeneration. Tilak's writing style continues to inspire scholars, philosophers, and activists alike, resonating with its timeless relevance and profound insights into human spirituality and societal ethics.

Audience engagement and accessibility

Dnyaneshwari employs storytelling and philosophical discourse to engage its audience, appealing to their emotions and intellect. Sant Dnyaneshwar addresses both spiritual seekers and the general public, offering a profound yet accessible interpretation of the Gita's teachings in the provincial language of Marathi. His commentary resonates with readers through its lyrical beauty and transformative potential, encouraging introspection and spiritual growth. Tilak's Gita Rahasya is aimed at a scholarly and politically aware audience, seeking to mobilize Indians towards the cause of national liberation. His commentary serves as a manifesto for social reform and political activism, using Gita's teachings to inspire a sense of duty (Karma) and sacrifice (Tyaga) among his readers. Tilak's strategic use of Sanskrit terminology and logical argumentation enhances the intellectual appeal of Gita Rahasya, positioning it as a seminal work in nationalist literature.

Commentary approaches

Dnyaneshwari adopts a holistic and inclusive approach to interpreting the Gita's teachings, synthesizing Bhakti (devotion) with Advaita Vedanta (monism) principles. Sant Dnyaneshwar emphasizes the unity of the individual soul (Jivatma) with the universal soul (Paramatma), presenting a vision of spiritual realization through love, devotion, and self-surrender. His commentary resonates with themes of divine grace, inner transformation, and the attainment of spiritual liberation

(Moksha). Tilak's Gita Rahasya focuses on the Gita's teachings on duty (Dharma) and action (Karma), interpreting them within the context of India's struggle against British colonial rule. Tilak advocates for a nationalist interpretation of the Gita, emphasizing the importance of selfless service and sacrifice in the pursuit of social justice and national liberation. His commentary highlights the ethical imperative of righteous action (Karma Yoga) and the role of individual agency in shaping historical destiny.

Dnyaneshwari contextualizes the Gita's teachings within the socio-cultural milieu of medieval Maharashtra, drawing upon local myths, legends, and religious traditions to illustrate spiritual truths. Sant Dnyaneshwar adapts the timeless wisdom of the Gita to resonate with the lived experiences of his audience, fostering a sense of cultural pride and spiritual awakening among the people of Maharashtra.

Tilak's Gita Rahasya situates the Gita's teachings within the context of British colonialism and India's struggle for independence. Tilak interprets Krishna's dialogue with Arjuna as a metaphor for the moral and political dilemmas faced by Indians under colonial rule, advocating for a revival of national consciousness and collective action. His commentary invokes historical references and cultural symbols to galvanize readers toward the cause of national liberation and social reform.

Interpretation of Social and Ethical Issues

Dnyaneshwari emphasizes the principles of righteousness (Dharma), compassion, and ethical conduct as essential aspects of spiritual practice. Sant Dnyaneshwar advocates for social harmony and moral integrity, using the Gita's teachings to promote a vision of a just and compassionate society. His commentary inspires individuals to align their actions with higher ethical principles and spiritual ideals, fostering a sense of communal solidarity and ethical responsibility.

Tilak's Gita Rahasya addresses issues of social justice, political ethics, and national duty in the context of colonial oppression. Tilak interprets Krishna's teachings on duty and sacrifice as a call to resist injustice and uphold the principles of selflessness and moral courage. His commentary challenges readers to confront social inequalities and systemic injustices, advocating for a transformative vision of national renewal and social reform.

Conclusion

The comparative literary analysis of Dnyaneshwari by Sant Dnyaneshwar and Gita Rahasya by Bal Gangadhar Tilak reveals profound insights into both the texts and their respective authors. Dnyaneshwari, characterized by its poetic depth and cultural richness, exemplifies Dnyaneshwar's ability to blend spiritual wisdom with accessible language and vivid imagery. His use of metaphors, colloquialisms, and the Ovi meter not only reveals the teachings of the Bhagavad Gita but also connects deeply with the cultural fabric of medieval Maharashtra. In contrast, Tilak's Gita Rahasya stands as a scholarly interpretation intertwined with nationalist fervour, offering insightful philosophical analysis and socio-political commentary. Tilak's writing style, marked by clarity, precision, and a nationalist perspective, underlines his vision for India's spiritual and societal regeneration through the teachings of the Gita. Both works, while distinct in their approaches and contexts, continue to resonate as timeless classics, inspiring seekers of knowledge and spiritual truth across generations and cultures. Ultimately, the comparative study of Dnyaneshwari and Gita Rahasya enriches our understanding of Hindu philosophy, literature, and the enduring relevance of the Bhagavad Gita's teachings in shaping spiritual, intellectual, and national identities.

However, even with limited exposure to the two texts, one can easily infer that the literary styles deployed in Dnyaneshwari by Sant

Dnyaneshwar and Gita Rahasya by Bal Gangadhar Tilak, while distinct in many respects, converge in several significant ways, reflecting their shared reverence for the Bhagavad Gita and their respective cultural contexts. Despite their stylistic differences, both works aim to interpret Gita's teachings on dharma (duty), moksha (liberation), and the nature of the self (Atman). Both, Dnyaneshwari, and Gita Rahasya reflect their respective cultural contexts through dialectal expression and literary devices. Both Dnyaneshwari and Gita Rahasya adopt interpretative approaches that blend spiritual insight with practical guidance that resonate with their respective audiences. The convergence of literary styles in Dnyaneshwari and Gita Rahasya lies in their enduring impact on Hindu philosophy, literature, and nationalist thought. Both works exemplify the transformative power of the Bhagavad Gita's teachings, fostering a deeper understanding of human existence, moral values, and the quest for spiritual enlightenment. To summarize, while Dnyaneshwari and Gita Rahasya employ distinct literary styles and interpretative approaches, they converge in their reverence for the Bhagavad Gita and their profound exploration of its timeless wisdom. Together, they enrich our understanding of Hindu philosophy, spirituality, and the enduring relevance of the Gita's teachings in navigating the complexities of human life and society.

Author's Notes:

Linguistics plays a pivotal role in understanding and analysing literature, offering insights into how language functions as a tool for expression, meaning-making, and cultural representation. By applying linguistic theories and methodologies, scholars delve into the intricate relationship between language and literature, revealing deeper layers of interpretation and significance. One fundamental aspect of linguistics in literature is stylistics, which examines how linguistic choices such as syntax, diction, and figurative language contribute to the aesthetic and emotional impact of literary texts. The stylistic analysis allows scholars to uncover patterns of language use unique to individual authors or literary movements, illuminating themes, characterization, and narrative structure (Carter, 2004).

Furthermore, sociolinguistics provides a lens through which literature reflects and critiques societal norms, identities, and power dynamics. Analysing linguistic variation and discourse patterns within texts can reveal how authors portray social hierarchies, regional dialects, or marginalized voices, thereby enriching our understanding of cultural diversity and social commentary in literature (Milroy & Milroy, 1999). In addition, pragmatics examines how context influences meaning in literary discourse. It explores the use of implicature, speech acts, and conversational implicature to decipher the intentions behind characters' dialogues or narrators' perspectives. Pragmatic analysis helps unravel layers of irony, ambiguity, and indirect communication in literature, shedding light on the complexities of interpersonal relationships and narrative reliability (Levinson, 1983). Moreover, cognitive linguistics offers insights into how readers comprehend and interpret literary texts through mental processes such as metaphorical reasoning, conceptual blending, and narrative schemas (Gibbs, 1994). By studying cognitive mechanisms involved in literary reception, scholars gain a deeper appreciation of how language shapes readers' engagement with narratives and emotional responses to fictional worlds.

Overall, linguistics serves as a powerful interdisciplinary tool for analysing literature, offering diverse perspectives on language structure, usage, and cultural context. By applying linguistic theories and methodologies, scholars uncover the intricate layers of meaning, stylistic devices, and socio-cultural implications embedded within literary texts, enriching our appreciation of literature's aesthetic, cognitive, and social dimensions.

References

Carter, R. (2004). *Language and Creativity: The Art of Common Talk*. Routledge.

Gibbs, R. W. (1994). *The Poetics of Mind: Figurative Thought, Language, and Understanding*. Cambridge University Press.

Levinson, S. C. (1983). *Pragmatics*. Cambridge University Press.

Milroy, L., & Milroy, J. (1999). *Authority in Language: Investigating Language Prescription and Standardisation*. Routledge.

Francine Prose (2009), Reading Like a Writer

Thomas Foster (2009), How to Read Literature Like a Professor

Chapter 5

Interpretation of Mythical Elements

Analysing the use of mythical elements by Dnyaneshwar and Tilak

---

"This drama(Hamlet) has portrayed in an excellent manner the state of mind of the young and tender-hearted Hamlet, who was faced with the puzzle as to whether he should put to death his sinful uncle and discharge his filial obligations towards his father, or pardon him, because he was his uncle, his step-father, as also the ruling king; and how he, later on, became, insane, because he did not find any proper path shower and guardian like Sri Krsna" – Lokmanya Tilak in Gita Rahasya (English Translation by B S Sukhtankar)

Concept of Myth

Myth in literature is a multifaceted concept that transcends mere storytelling; it embodies cultural, spiritual, and philosophical truths that resonate across generations and civilizations. Originating from ancient oral traditions and evolving through literary forms, myths in literature serve various functions, from explaining natural phenomena to elucidating moral codes and exploring existential questions. Myth can be defined as a traditional narrative that typically involves gods, heroes, and supernatural beings. These narratives often explain the origins of the world, natural phenomena, customs, rituals, and societal values. Mythical stories are passed down orally or through written texts and play a crucial role in shaping cultural identities and belief systems.

Myths frequently employ symbolic language and allegorical narratives to convey deeper meanings. Characters and events represent universal archetypes and moral dilemmas that transcend specific contexts. Myths are rooted in specific cultural and historical contexts, reflecting the values, beliefs, and social structures of the societies that produce them. However, they often contain elements that resonate across cultures and time periods. Mythical narratives evolve through oral tradition and literary adaptation. They may undergo reinterpretation and transformation to suit changing cultural norms and audience expectations while retaining their core thematic elements. Myths can straddle the line between the sacred and the profane. They may serve religious or spiritual purposes, offering explanations for the mysteries of existence and guiding ethical behaviour. At the same time, myths can entertain and inspire imagination through fantastical tales of heroism and adventure.

Myths often provide origin stories for the universe, natural phenomena (such as the sun and moon), and human customs (such as marriage and burial rites). These narratives offer a sense of order and purpose to the world. Mythical narratives convey moral lessons and ethical principles through the actions and fates of their characters. They reinforce societal norms and values, teaching virtues such as courage, loyalty, and justice. Myths play a crucial role in defining cultural identity and preserving collective memory. They reinforce a sense of belonging and continuity across generations, connecting individuals to their cultural heritage. Myths explore the depths of human experience, exploring existential questions about life, death, fate, and the nature of reality. They provide frameworks for understanding the human condition and grappling with existential uncertainties. Mythical motifs and themes continue to inspire writers and artists across genres. They provide rich sources of symbolism and narrative structure that resonate with contemporary audiences. Myths transcend cultural boundaries, resonating with diverse audiences around the world. They serve as points of connection and comparison across different civilizations, highlighting universal themes and human experiences. Scholars and literary critics analyse myths to uncover hidden meanings, cultural values, and psychological insights. Mythical narratives invite multiple interpretations, reflecting the complexity and depth of human storytelling. Myths are continually adapted and modernized in literature, film, theatre, and other artistic mediums. These adaptations reinterpret ancient narratives for contemporary audiences while retaining their fundamental themes and motifs.

Myth in literature encompasses narratives that blend imagination with cultural significance, serving as repositories of collective wisdom, identity, and moral guidance. From ancient epics to modern novels, myths continue to evolve and resonate, offering timeless insights into the human experience and reflecting the enduring power of storytelling. Understanding myth in literature enriches our appreciation of cultural diversity, historical continuity, and the universal themes that unite humanity across time and space. As such, myths remain integral to the fabric of literary tradition and continue to shape our understanding of the world and ourselves. Roland Barthes, a prominent French philosopher, literary theorist, and semiotician, introduced a ground-breaking perspective on myths in his influential work titled "Mythologies," published in 1957. Barthes' exploration of myths challenges traditional notions by suggesting that myths are not merely ancient stories or legends but are also pervasive ideological constructs embedded in contemporary culture.

Mythical elements in world literature

Mythical elements have permeated world literature for centuries, enriching narratives with symbolic depth, cultural significance, and timeless appeal. Here are some of the most remarkable examples prominently featured in non-Indian literature:

Homer's epic poems, the *Iliad,* and the *Odyssey*, are foundational works of Western literature that incorporate a wealth of Greek mythical elements. Heroes like Achilles, Hector, and Odysseus navigate the whims of gods and goddesses such as Zeus, Athena, and Poseidon, embodying human virtues and flaws against a backdrop of divine intervention and epic battles.

Snorri Sturluson's *Prose Edda* is a collection of Old Norse mythological stories and poems that provides a comprehensive account of Norse mythology and cosmology. It includes tales of gods like Odin, Thor, and Loki, as well as epic narratives of creation, heroism, and the prophesied end of the world (Ragnarök).

Sir Thomas Malory's *Le Morte d 'Arthur* is a compilation of medieval tales and romances centred around King Arthur, the Knights of the Round Table, and the quest for the Holy Grail. These legends are steeped in mythical elements such as magical swords (Excalibur), sorcery (Merlin), and quests that explore themes of chivalry, honour, and destiny.

One Thousand and One Nights, a classic of Middle Eastern folk tales features a rich confluence of mythical and supernatural elements woven into stories such as "Aladdin's Wonderful Lamp," "Ali Baba and the Forty Thieves," and "Sinbad the Sailor." Magical beings, jinn, and enchanted objects form integral parts of these tales, highlighting themes of fate, trickery, and moral lessons.

Murasaki Shikibu's 11th-century masterpiece, *The Tale of Genji*, draws upon Japanese mythology and courtly traditions to portray the life and love of its protagonist, Prince Genji. Spirits (kami), divine interventions, and rituals play significant roles in shaping the narrative and reflecting cultural beliefs about beauty, fate, and the supernatural.

Popol Vuh is an ancient Mayan text that recounts the creation myth, legendary tales, and the exploits of hero twins Hunahpu and Xbalanque. It explores themes of creation, heroism, and the struggle between gods and humans, embodying the rich cultural and spiritual heritage of the Maya civilization.

These examples demonstrate how mythical elements have been used across diverse cultures and epochs to convey universal truths, explore human experiences, and impart moral and philosophical insights that resonate with readers worldwide. They continue to inspire and captivate audiences, highlighting the enduring power of mythology in shaping literary traditions and cultural identities.

Politics of myth

The politics behind myths encapsulates the ways in which mythical narratives are constructed, propagated, and utilized to influence social, cultural, and political dynamics within societies. This description inquiries into how myths are integrally intertwined with power dynamics, ideology formation, and governance strategies across different historical and cultural contexts. Myths are often crafted to serve specific political agendas and interests. Rulers, religious leaders, and cultural elites have historically employed myths to legitimize their authority and justify their rule. For instance, in ancient civilizations like Egypt and Mesopotamia, rulers claimed divine lineage or favour through myths, portraying themselves as intermediaries between the gods and the people. This divine sanction enhanced their political legitimacy and consolidated their power over subjects. Myths contribute to ideological hegemony by reinforcing dominant beliefs, values, and norms within societies. They naturalize social hierarchies, justify inequalities, and uphold the status quo. For example, in feudal Europe, myths such as the "divine right of kings" affirmed the absolute authority of monarchs and discouraged challenges to their rule. Similarly, myths of racial superiority have been used to justify colonialism, slavery, and discriminatory practices by perpetuating stereotypes and hierarchies of human worth.

Myths play an important role in nation-building by fostering a sense of collective identity and shared destiny among citizens. National myths often celebrate heroic figures, foundational events, and cultural achievements that symbolize the values and aspirations of a nation. For instance, myths of independence and resilience are central to the national narratives of many post-colonial countries, inspiring patriotism, and unity among diverse populations. Myths can be employed as tools of propaganda to sway public opinion, justify policies, and mobilize support for political agendas. Governments, political parties, and interest groups utilize myths through media, education, and public discourse to shape perceptions, cultivate loyalty, and garner legitimacy. This strategic use of myths is evident in campaigns promoting national security, economic prosperity, or social welfare initiatives. Despite their role in reinforcing power structures, myths can also be contested, subverted, or reinterpreted to challenge authority and promote social change. Counter-myths or alternative narratives emerge to critique dominant ideologies, expose injustices, and advocate for marginalized communities. For example, movements for civil rights, gender equality, and environmental justice often draw on myths of liberation, empowerment, and solidarity to mobilize grassroots support and challenge entrenched inequalities. In contemporary society, the politics behind myths continue to evolve in response to globalization, digital media, and cultural diversity. The proliferation of information technologies has democratized the creation and dissemination of myths, allowing diverse voices and perspectives to be heard. However, the manipulation of myths through disinformation campaigns, conspiracy theories, and ideological polarization underlines the ongoing relevance of understanding the political dimensions of mythmaking. The politics behind myths reveals their role in shaping ideologies, identities, and power relations within societies. Whether used to consolidate authority, maintain social order, or mobilize resistance, myths embody complex narratives that reflect and influence political realities. By critically examining the construction, dissemination, and contested interpretations of myths, we gain insights into the dynamics of power, ideology, and social change that continue to shape our collective understanding of the world. Understanding the politics behind myths is essential for navigating contemporary challenges and advancing inclusive narratives that promote justice, equality, and human dignity.

The politics of myth in religious sacred texts encompasses the complex interplay between spiritual narratives and socio-political authority within religious traditions. These texts, revered as divine revelations or teachings, often serve dual roles: they impart spiritual guidance and moral teachings while also legitimizing religious hierarchies and governance structures. Myths within religious scriptures frequently uphold theological doctrines, moral precepts, and rituals that reinforce the authority of religious institutions and leaders. They shape collective beliefs, values, and practices among followers, fostering cohesion and identity within religious communities. Moreover, the interpretation and dissemination of these myths can be politicized to advance agendas of social control, cultural hegemony, and even geopolitical influence. As such, the politics of myth in religious sacred texts illuminates how spiritual narratives intersect with power dynamics, ideology formation, and social order, shaping both individual faith and broader societal norms.

Mythical elements in the Bhagavad Gita

I

Mythical elements are at the centre of Bhagavad Gita around which Vyasa weaves his profound philosophical teachings. One of the primary mythical elements in the Bhagavad Gita, and perhaps one of the most remarkable mythical elements ever, is the divine incarnation of Krishna. Krishna is portrayed as both a human and as a divine figure, embodying the principles of dharma and acting as a guide and mentor to Arjuna. The concept of avatars, or divine incarnations, is central to Hindu mythology and is exemplified in Krishna's presence in the Gita. His avataric form serves as a reminder of the eternal cycle of birth and rebirth (sansara) and the divine intervention in human affairs to restore cosmic balance (dharma). Krishna's manifestation as both a human and a god blurs the lines between the mortal and the divine, underscoring the mystical and mythical dimensions of his character.

Another mythical element in the Bhagavad Gita is the symbolism surrounding Arjuna's chariot. The chariot represents the body as a vehicle for the soul, with Krishna as the charioteer guiding Arjuna through the battlefield of life. This imagery conveys the idea of the spiritual journey and the importance of aligning one's actions (the horses) with higher spiritual wisdom (the charioteer) to achieve liberation (moksha). The dialogue between Arjuna and Krishna unfolds amidst the backdrop of the Kurukshetra war, a legendary battle between the Pandavas and the Kauravas. This war serves as a metaphorical conflict between righteousness (dharma) and unrighteousness (adharma), highlighting the eternal struggle between good and evil in the cosmic order. The battlefield becomes a mythical stage where moral dilemmas are played out and where divine intervention shapes the course of human destiny. The Gita expounds on the concepts of karma (action) and reincarnation (sansara), which are fundamental to Hindu mythology and cosmology. The idea that actions have consequences across lifetimes and that the soul undergoes cycles of birth and rebirth clarifies the mythical notion of the eternal journey of the soul toward spiritual evolution and ultimate liberation.

Mythical elements in the Bhagavad Gita are not merely ornamental; they serve to elucidate profound spiritual truths and ethical principles. The recurring motifs of divine incarnation, cosmic symbolism, and metaphorical warfare contribute to the Gita's enduring appeal and relevance across cultures and epochs. The Gita's mythical dimensions enrich its philosophical teachings, providing a framework for understanding the complexities of human existence and the pursuit of spiritual enlightenment. The Gita incorporates various mythical elements that enhance its narrative and philosophical depth. Through the divine incarnation of Krishna, the symbolism of the chariot, and the metaphorical backdrop of the Kurukshetra war, the Gita conveys profound spiritual teachings while drawing on rich mythological imagery. These mythical elements not only enrich the text but also resonate with universal themes of duty, devotion, and the eternal quest for self-realization.

II

Vyasa strategically employed mythical elements to convey profound philosophical teachings and engage the reader on multiple levels. His use of mythology in the Bhagavad Gita can be understood through several political, cultural, and literary lenses.

One rationale of Vyasa behind the use of these elements could be to achieve cultural relevance and accessibility. In ancient Indian society, mythology played a crucial role in conveying complex philosophical ideas in a way that was accessible and relatable to people from diverse backgrounds. By embedding deep spiritual teachings within familiar mythical narratives, Vyasa ensured that the Bhagavad Gita would resonate with a wide audience, from scholars to common folk, thereby fostering a broader understanding and acceptance of its teachings.

Mythology often serves to legitimize authority and impart moral and ethical teachings through narratives that blend historical events with supernatural elements. In the Bhagavad Gita, Krishna's divine incarnation as both a god and a charioteer for Arjuna serves to legitimize Krishna's authority as a spiritual guide and teacher of profound truths. This divine authority helps reinforce the moral and ethical principles Krishna imparts to Arjuna, thereby strengthening their impact on the listener or reader.

The Mahabharata, of which the Bhagavad Gita is a part, is not merely an epic but also a reflection of political dynamics and struggles for power in ancient India. The use of mythology in the Gita, particularly the dialogue on the battlefield of Kurukshetra, serves as a metaphorical commentary on the dilemmas faced by rulers and leaders in governance. The ethical and moral dilemmas faced by Arjuna, representing a righteous prince torn between duty and compassion, reflect broader political concerns about governance, justice, and the responsibilities of rulers.

Mythical elements in the Bhagavad Gita are also employed to convey universal moral principles that transcend time and place. The cosmic symbolism of Arjuna's chariot, guided by Krishna, symbolizes the eternal struggle between good and evil, duty and desire, which resonates with audiences across cultures and epochs. By grounding these principles in mythical narratives, Vyasa ensured their enduring relevance and applicability to diverse human experiences.

Mythology in the Bhagavad Gita is intricately linked to concepts of spiritual evolution (self-realization) and liberation (moksha). The teachings on karma, reincarnation, and devotion (bhakti) are conveyed through mythical narratives that illustrate the transformative journey of the soul toward spiritual enlightenment. Mythology thus serves as a vehicle for exploring profound existential questions about the nature of reality, the purpose of life, and the attainment of ultimate liberation.

To conclude, Vyasa's use of mythical elements in the Bhagavad Gita serves multiple purposes, including cultural accessibility, the legitimization of spiritual authority, political allegory, conveying universal moral principles, and exploring profound spiritual truths. Through these elements, Vyasa crafted a timeless philosophical discourse that continues to inspire and guide seekers of wisdom and truth across the world.

Mythical elements in Dnyaneshwari and Gita Rahasya – a comparative

I

Dnyaneshwari employs a blend of direct commentary and mythical narratives to explain the Gita's teachings. It uses stories and allegories from Hindu mythology to illustrate concepts such as karma, dharma, and devotion. Tilak, a scholar, and nationalist leader, examines the Gita in the context of India's struggle for independence from British rule, infusing his commentary with socio-political interpretations.

Similar to the Gita itself, Krishna in Dnyaneshwari is depicted as the divine charioteer and teacher who imparts spiritual wisdom to Arjuna. Dnyaneshwari incorporates mythical allegories and stories to elaborate on philosophical concepts. For example, stories of gods and sages are used to illustrate the principles of devotion (bhakti) and the path of self-realization. Unlike Dnyaneshwari, Gita Rahasya uses mythical elements more as historical and political allegories. Tilak interprets Krishna's teachings to Arjuna as symbolic of moral duty and righteous action in the face of social and political challenges. Krishna's role in Gita Rahasya is depicted as a guide who advocates for social justice and moral integrity, reflecting Tilak's interpretation of Gita's relevance to contemporary socio-political issues.

Dnyaneshwari emphasizes the inward journey of the soul towards union with the divine, drawing on transcendental elements to illustrate the transformative process of spiritual realization. Mythical elements in Dnyaneshwari are used to convey universal spiritual truths that transcend cultural and historical contexts, making the teachings of the Gita accessible to a broader audience. Gita Rahasya employs mythical elements to address contemporary issues such as governance, nationalism, and social reform. It emphasizes the practical application of the Gita's teachings in everyday life and societal contexts.

II

While both texts utilize mythical elements to interpret the Bhagavad Gita, Dnyaneshwari focuses more on spiritual and devotional aspects, using myths to illustrate universal spiritual truths. In contrast, Gita Rahasya employs myths as allegories to address socio-political issues and moral dilemmas. Dnyaneshwari emphasizes the inner spiritual journey and the individual's quest for self-realization, whereas Gita Rahasya emphasizes the Gita's relevance to societal and political challenges, advocating for righteous action and social justice. Dnyaneshwari, written in Marathi, aims for accessibility to a wider audience through devotional and philosophical insights. Gita Rahasya, targets scholars and intellectuals, focusing on socio-political interpretations and practical applications. Their comparative analysis highlights the diversity of interpretations and applications of the Gita's teachings across different historical, cultural, and philosophical contexts.

Author's Notes:

Myths often transcend their surface narratives to address the depths of human experience. For instance, the Kurukshetra War in the Bhagavad Gita symbolizes the internal battle between duty and desire, mirroring Carl Jung's concept of the *shadow*—the hidden aspects of the self (Jung, *Psychological Aspects of the Persona*). Similarly, Greek myths like the labours of Hercules can be seen as symbolic journeys through the hero's psychological struggles and personal growth, aligning with Joseph Campbell's idea of the *hero's journey* as an archetypal quest for self-discovery (Campbell, *The Hero with a Thousand Faces*).

References

The documentary "Joseph Campell and Power of Myth" on YouTube – episode one to episode 6 (1988), PBS.

This interesting documentary captures conversations between mythologist Joseph Campbell and journalist Bill Moyers about the role of myth in society. A brief synopsis of episodes is as under:

Ep 1: Discussion on cultural heroes like Krishna, Buddha, and Jesus and their journeys

Ep 2: How myths reveal spiritual potential

Ep 3: Powerful role of myth in early hunting societies

Ep 4: About death, sacrifice, and rebirth in agricultural cultures and the idea that there are `hidden hands' guiding life's work.

Ep 5: Romance, the Holy Grail, marriage, and the symbolism of the virgin birth.

Ep 6: Contrast in Eastern and Western religions and exploring the meaning of life and suffering.

Radhakrishnan, S. (Ed.). (1994). *The Bhagavadgītā*

Sargeant, W. (2009). *The Bhagavad Gita: Twenty-fifth–Anniversary Edition*

Zaehner, R. C. (1973). *The Bhagavad-Gītā: or The Lord's Song*

Chapter 6

Spiritual and Ethical Dimensions

Deep dive into the spiritual and ethical dimensions in Dnyaneshwari and Gita Rahasya

Spiritual Dimensions - Dnyaneshwari

I

Foundations of the spiritual edifice of Dnyaneshwari are built on the monistic philosophy of Advaita Vedanta. Dnyaneshwari emphasizes the monistic philosophy (Advaita Vedanta) where the individual soul (jivatma) is seen as the same as the universal soul (Paramatma) or

Brahman. The influence of monism on Dnyaneshwar is unambiguously manifested in Dnyaneshwari.

Advaita Vedanta, or monistic Vedanta, is a school of Hindu philosophy that advances the ultimate reality (Brahman) as indivisible, transcendent, and beyond all forms of differentiation. It asserts that the individual soul (jivatma) is fundamentally identical to Brahman, and the perceived duality between them is due to ignorance (avidya). Liberation (moksha) is achieved through self-realization of this non-duality, often through methods such as self-inquiry (jnana yoga), meditation (dhyana), and devotion (bhakti). Dnyaneshwar, influenced by the teachings of his spiritual lineage (Nath tradition) and his profound understanding of Vedantic texts, particularly the Upanishads and the Bhagavad Gita, synthesized these teachings into a coherent framework in Dnyaneshwari. His interpretation of monism is not merely theoretical but deeply experiential, reflecting his spiritual realization and the transformative impact it had on his life and teachings.

Dnyaneshwari expounds on the teachings of the Bhagavad Gita, chapter by chapter, offering profound insights into the nature of existence, the paths to liberation, and the relationship between the individual and the universal. At its core, Dnyaneshwari emphasizes the key philosophical tenets of monism. Dnyaneshwar consistently stresses the unity of all beings in Brahman, dismantling the illusion of separateness caused by ignorance. He explains how the true nature of the self (atman) is beyond distinctions and limitations imposed by the physical world. Drawing from monism, Dnyaneshwari discusses the concept of Maya (illusion) and avidya (ignorance), which veil the true nature of reality. Through clear and insightful commentary, he guides the reader towards recognizing and transcending these illusions to realize the eternal truth. Central to the philosophy of monism is the notion of self-realization (atma-jnana), wherein one recognizes oneself as not merely an individual entity but as the unchanging, eternal essence that is Brahman. Dnyaneshwar's commentary encourages introspection and inner inquiry as means to attain this realization. While firmly rooted in the philosophy of monism, Dnyaneshwari also integrates elements of devotion (bhakti). This synthesis is characteristic of Dnyaneshwar's approach, wherein the intellectual pursuit of knowledge (jnana) and the emotional surrender to divine grace (bhakti) are seen as complementary paths to spiritual liberation. He emphasizes the transformative power of devotion in purifying the mind and preparing it for the direct experience of Brahman.

Despite its foundational monistic roots, Dnyaneshwari allows for various interpretations and philosophical explorations. Different commentators and scholars have approached Dnyaneshwari from different perspectives, emphasizing either the monist elements or the devotional aspects, depending on their own spiritual inclinations and philosophical leanings.

II

The influence of the Bhakti tradition on Sant Dnyaneshwar and his magnum opus, Dnyaneshwari, represents a profound intersection of devotion, spiritual insight, and philosophical depth within the context of medieval Maharashtra. Bhakti, often translated as devotion or loving surrender to the divine, is a spiritual path that emphasizes a personal and emotional connection with the divine. It transcends mere ritualistic worship and external observances, focusing instead on a deep longing for union with the divine through love and surrender. The Bhakti movement in medieval India, including Maharashtra, sought to democratize spirituality by making it accessible to all individuals regardless of caste or social status. This movement found expression in various regional languages, including Marathi, through devotional poetry, songs, and philosophical treatises.

Dnyaneshwar was born into a family of saints and scholars in Maharashtra, during a period marked by religious and social reforms initiated by the Bhakti movement. Influenced by his family's Nath tradition and his own spiritual experiences, Dnyaneshwar integrated Bhakti seamlessly into his philosophical framework. Unlike some other Vedantic philosophers who emphasized intellectual inquiry and renunciation, Dnyaneshwar emphasized the role of heartfelt devotion (bhakti) as a means to spiritual realization. Dnyaneshwari is not only a philosophical commentary but also a work of poetic beauty. Dnyaneshwar's mastery of the Marathi language allowed him to express profound spiritual truths in a language accessible to the common people. His verses are infused with bhakti, evoking deep emotional responses, and fostering a sense of intimacy with the divine. Through his poetic expression, Dnyaneshwar conveyed the essence of Bhakti—love, surrender, and longing for union with God. One of the hallmarks of the Bhakti movement was its emphasis on inclusivity and accessibility. Dnyaneshwar's decision to compose Dnyaneshwari in Marathi, the language of the people, rather than in Sanskrit, symbolizes his commitment to making spiritual knowledge available to everyone. This democratization of spirituality was revolutionary for its time, empowering individuals from all social classes to engage directly with the teachings of the Bhagavad Gita and Advaita Vedanta through the lens of Bhakti. Dnyaneshwari harmoniously integrates the paths of knowledge (jnana), devotion (bhakti), and action (karma) prescribed in the Bhagavad Gita. While elucidating the philosophical depths of monism, Dnyaneshwar emphasizes that bhakti is not separate from knowledge but rather a natural expression of love and devotion towards the ultimate truth, which is Brahman. In Dnyaneshwari, Dnyaneshwar frequently underlines the importance of surrendering one's ego and desires to the divine will. He portrays bhakti as a transformative force that purifies the mind and prepares it for the direct experience of Brahman. Through examples, metaphors, and lyrical verses, Dnyaneshwari inspires readers to cultivate an unwavering devotion to God as the path to liberation. Beyond theoretical discussions, Dnyaneshwari offers practical guidance on how to cultivate bhakti in everyday life. Dnyaneshwar encourages devotees to engage in selfless service (seva), chanting of sacred mantras, and contemplation on the divine attributes as ways to deepen their devotion and spiritual progress. His teachings emphasize the transformative power of bhakti in overcoming the obstacles of Maya (illusion) and Avidya (ignorance) on the path to self-realization.

Ethical Dimensions – Dnyaneshwari

I

Ethical conduct, as elaborated in Dnyaneshwari by Sant Dnyaneshwar, emerges as a foundational aspect of his spiritual teachings and commentary on the Bhagavad Gita. Righteous duty, non-violence, truthfulness, non-stealing, purity, and non-attachment are the key principles of ethical conduct upheld by Dnyaneshwar.

Dnyaneshwari places significant emphasis on Dharma, which encompasses righteous duty, moral responsibility, and ethical conduct. The concept of Dharma is central to Hindu philosophy and is discussed extensively in the Bhagavad Gita, which Dnyaneshwari elucidates. Ethical conduct, therefore, involves aligning one's actions with Dharma, which varies according to one's role and station in life (varna and Ashrama). Dnyaneshwari stresses the importance of non-violence towards all beings. Sant Dnyaneshwar highlights that violence arises from ignorance and egoism, perpetuating cycles of suffering. Ahimsa is not just physical non-violence but extends to thoughts and words, promoting harmony and compassion in all interactions. Truthfulness is another cornerstone of ethical conduct in Dnyaneshwari. Sant Dnyaneshwar emphasizes the importance of speaking the truth in all circumstances, as falsehood leads to confusion and discord. Satya is seen as an essential virtue that aligns with the spiritual path of self-realization. Asteya, or non-stealing, is highlighted as a moral imperative in Dnyaneshwari. Sant Dnyaneshwar condemns theft and dishonesty in all forms, recognizing that stealing disrupts the social order and erodes trust among individuals. Practicing Asteya fosters integrity and respect for others' property and rights. The purity of mind and body is emphasized in Dnyaneshwari as essential for spiritual progress. Sant Dnyaneshwar discusses the purification of one's thoughts, intentions, and actions through self-discipline and adherence to ethical principles. Shoucha involves maintaining cleanliness, both externally and internally, to cultivate clarity and inner peace. Aparigraha, or non-attachment to material possessions and desires, is advocated in Dnyaneshwari as a means to overcome selfishness and greed. Sant Dnyaneshwar teaches that attachment binds individuals to the cycle of birth and death (sansara), hindering spiritual evolution. Practicing Aparigraha fosters detachment and contentment, leading to inner freedom and spiritual growth. Dnyaneshwari extensively explores the concept of Karma Yoga, which is the path of selfless action performed with dedication and without attachment to the results. Sant Dnyaneshwar emphasizes that ethical conduct is integral to Karma Yoga, as actions performed in accordance with Dharma and for the well-being of others purify the mind and lead to spiritual liberation. By fulfilling one's duties (svadharma) with sincerity and integrity, individuals contribute positively to society and progress on the path of self-realization.

While Dnyaneshwari provides a comprehensive framework for ethical conduct, some critiques may argue that its emphasis on duty and moral responsibility could potentially overshadow the principle of compassion and empathy towards all beings. The text's focus on upholding social order and adherence to Dharma might be perceived as conservative or rigid by those advocating for more flexible moral frameworks that prioritize individual freedom and subjective ethical choices. However, maintaining a matured perspective can help one appreciate that it is not a zero-sum game after all, and Dnyaneshwari indeed creates a mental ambience that can strike a right balance between duty and compassion.

II

While enlightening the reader on Karma Yoga, Dnyaneshwari particularly attaches to it the element of ethical conduct. Dnyaneshwari underlines the importance of performing actions selflessly, without attachment to the results. This ethical stance promotes a mindset where individuals focus on the process and intent behind their actions rather than solely on achieving personal gain or gratification. By cultivating selflessness, Karma Yoga encourages individuals to contribute positively to society and uphold moral values such as compassion and service.

Central to Karma Yoga in Dnyaneshwari is the concept of Dharma, or righteous duty. Sant Dnyaneshwar emphasizes the ethical imperative of fulfilling one's duties (svadharma) according to one's role and station in life (varna and ashrama). This integration of ethical conduct with Dharma ensures that actions are performed with integrity and adherence to moral principles, thereby contributing to social harmony and collective well-being. Karma Yoga, as elucidated in Dnyaneshwari, serves as a path for purifying the mind and intentions of the practitioner. By engaging in actions without egoism and attachment, individuals transcend selfish desires and cultivate virtues such as humility, patience, and generosity. This ethical purification not only facilitates personal growth but also fosters a deeper sense of unity and empathy towards others. Dnyaneshwari presents Karma Yoga as a universally applicable path to spiritual liberation, accessible to individuals from all social classes. Its ethical dimensions emphasize that ethical conduct and spiritual progress are not limited to renunciants or scholars but are attainable through sincere engagement in one's responsibilities and service to others. This inclusive approach accentuates the practicality and relevance of Karma Yoga in contemporary ethical discourse.

III

While Dnyaneshwari advocates for the fulfilment of duties (svadharma), there is a potential critique that this emphasis on duty-bound action might lead to a rigid adherence to societal norms and roles, limiting individual creativity and autonomy. Critics argue that an excessive focus on duty could suppress individual expression and the exploration of alternative ethical frameworks that prioritize personal growth and well-being. Karma Yoga, as described in Dnyaneshwari, emphasizes action as a means to spiritual realization. However, there is a critique that this emphasis on constant engagement in worldly activities might neglect the importance of introspection, contemplation, and inner silence as essential aspects of ethical and spiritual development. Critics argue for a more balanced approach that integrates both active engagement in the world and periods of contemplative practice. While Karma Yoga promotes detachment from the fruits of actions (phala-tyaga), critics argue that achieving true detachment is challenging in practical terms. The ethical dimension of Karma Yoga requires individuals to perform actions without desire for personal gain or recognition, which can be difficult to maintain consistently in the face of societal pressures and personal ambitions. Critics suggest that a nuanced understanding of detachment is necessary, one that acknowledges the complexities of human motivations and aspirations. Dnyaneshwari's ethical dimensions of Karma Yoga primarily focus on personal ethics and spiritual growth. Critics argue that while personal ethics are fundamental, Karma Yoga could further explore its implications for social justice and systemic inequalities. Addressing ethical dimensions in the context of collective responsibility and advocacy for social change could enhance the relevance of Karma Yoga in addressing contemporary ethical challenges.

Dnyaneshwari's exposition of Karma Yoga provides invaluable insights into ethical conduct and spiritual practice, emphasizing selfless action, ethical integrity, and the pursuit of spiritual liberation. While acknowledging its strengths in promoting moral virtues and ethical living, a critical examination reveals areas where deeper exploration and refinement could enhance its ethical dimensions. By addressing critiques and further exploring the complexities of ethical conduct within Karma Yoga, Dnyaneshwari continues to offer timeless wisdom and practical guidance for individuals seeking ethical clarity and spiritual evolution.

Spiritual Dimensions – Gita Rahasya

I

Much like the Dnyaneshwari, Gita Rahasya underlines the importance of performing actions selflessly, without attachment to personal desires or outcomes. Tilak interprets Karma Yoga as a path to spiritual liberation through the diligent execution of one's duties (svadharma), while relinquishing attachment to the fruits of those actions (phala-tyaga). His emphasis is on guiding one's duties towards the welfare of people, society, and nation. Tilak integrates Karma Yoga seamlessly with the philosophy of monism, emphasizing the non-dualistic principle of unity (Brahman) underlying all existence. He interprets Krishna's teachings in the Gita as guiding individuals toward realizing their inherent divinity through selfless action and surrender to the divine will. This integration provides a comprehensive framework for understanding Karma Yoga as a transformative spiritual practice. Gita Rahasya offers practical insights into applying Karma Yoga principles in everyday life. Tilak discusses how individuals can cultivate mindfulness, ethical integrity, and resilience through Karma Yoga, thereby aligning their actions with higher spiritual ideals while contributing positively to society. This practical approach encourages readers to integrate spiritual teachings into their personal and professional lives, promoting holistic development and spiritual fulfilment. Tilak presents Karma Yoga as a universally accessible path to spiritual realization, applicable to individuals from diverse backgrounds and life circumstances. By emphasizing the universality of ethical conduct and spiritual growth through Karma Yoga, Gita Rahasya resonates with readers seeking deeper meaning, purpose, and transcendence in their lives. This inclusivity enhances the relevance of Karma Yoga in addressing contemporary spiritual dilemmas and existential quests.

II

While Gita Rahasya advocates for selfless action and duty-bound ethics, there is a potential critique that its emphasis on Karma Yoga might overshadow the importance of inner contemplation, meditation, and introspection as integral aspects of spiritual practice. Critics argue for a more balanced approach that acknowledges the complementary roles of active engagement (Karma Yoga) and passive receptivity (Jnana Yoga) in spiritual evolution. Tilak's interpretation of Karma Yoga emphasizes detachment from the results of actions (phala-tyaga) as a means to spiritual liberation. Critics argue that achieving true non-attachment is challenging in practical terms, especially in modern contexts where success, recognition, and material rewards often influence motivations. A nuanced understanding of detachment is necessary, one that acknowledges the complexities of human desires and aspirations without compromising ethical integrity. While Gita Rahasya explores the spiritual dimensions of Karma Yoga, critics contend that it could further elaborate on its implications for social justice and systemic inequalities. Addressing ethical dimensions in the context of collective responsibility and advocacy for social change would enhance the relevance of Karma Yoga in addressing contemporary ethical challenges and promoting inclusivity, compassion, and social harmony. Gita Rahasya reflects Tilak's nationalist interpretations and socio-political context, which influence his understanding of Karma Yoga and its spiritual dimensions. Critics argue that these interpretations may limit the universality of Karma Yoga's teachings and overlook diverse perspectives and interpretations within the Bhagavad Gita. A more inclusive approach that considers diverse cultural, philosophical, and spiritual traditions could enrich the discourse on Karma Yoga and its relevance in a globalized world.

Ethical Dimensions – Gita Rahasya

I

The ethical dimensions of Karma Yoga as described in Gita Rahasya by Bal Gangadhar Tilak present a unique interpretation of the Bhagavad Gita that intertwines ethical conduct with spiritual practice and nationalist fervour. Gita Rahasya emphasizes the importance of fulfilling one's duties (svadharma) with sincerity and integrity. Tilak interprets Karma Yoga as a path to spiritual liberation through selfless action performed in accordance with Dharma (righteous duty). This ethical stance promotes a sense of moral responsibility and ethical conduct, encouraging individuals to contribute positively to society while maintaining inner purity and selflessness. Tilak's interpretation of Karma Yoga in Gita Rahasya includes a nationalist perspective that emphasizes service to the nation (Rashtra Dharma) as a form of righteous action. This integration of ethical conduct with nationalist ethics encourages readers to align their actions with the welfare and progress of the nation, thereby fostering a sense of civic duty and patriotism. Tilak's advocacy for social reform and resistance against colonial oppression is framed within the ethical framework of Karma Yoga, motivating individuals to act for the greater good of society. Gita Rahasya offers practical insights into applying Karma Yoga principles in public life and governance. Tilak discusses how ethical leadership, integrity, and selflessness are essential for political and social reform. By emphasizing the ethical dimensions of Karma Yoga in the context of governance and public service, Tilak inspires individuals to integrate spiritual values into their roles as leaders and citizens, promoting ethical governance and societal well-being. Tilak interprets Karma Yoga as a means to cultivate ethical integrity and detachment from personal desires and ambitions. He advocates for non-attachment to the results of actions (phala-tyaga) as a pathway to inner peace and spiritual liberation. This ethical stance encourages individuals to perform their duties diligently while relinquishing attachment to outcomes, thereby promoting humility, resilience, and spiritual growth.

II

While Gita Rahasya emphasizes the importance of duty-bound ethics, there is a potential critique that its focus on adhering to societal norms and roles (svadharma) might lead to ethical rigidness. Critics argue that an overemphasis on duty could potentially stifle individual creativity, autonomy, and the exploration of alternative ethical frameworks that prioritize personal growth and well-being. Tilak's nationalist interpretation of Karma Yoga in Gita Rahasya focuses primarily on ethical conduct in service to the nation (Rashtra Dharma). Critics contend that this emphasis might overlook broader ethical considerations, such as global solidarity, environmental stewardship, and human rights, which are increasingly relevant in contemporary ethical discourse. A more inclusive approach that considers diverse ethical perspectives and universal values could enrich the ethical dimensions of Karma Yoga as presented in Gita Rahasya. Tilak's advocacy for ethical conduct in Gita Rahasya navigates the tension between pragmatic engagement in social and political spheres and the idealistic pursuit of spiritual liberation. Critics argue that balancing ethical pragmatism with spiritual idealism requires nuanced discernment and contextual sensitivity, especially in complex socio-political environments where ethical dilemmas and conflicting interests are prevalent. Gita Rahasya reflects Tilak's socio-political context and nationalist interpretations, which influence his understanding of Karma Yoga and its ethical dimensions. Critics suggest that these interpretations may limit the universality of Karma Yoga's ethical teachings and overlook diverse cultural, philosophical, and spiritual traditions. A more inclusive approach that acknowledges the plurality of ethical perspectives could broaden the discourse on Karma Yoga and its relevance in fostering global ethical awareness and harmony.

Difference in approach and yet converging messaging

The spiritual and ethical dimensions unfolded in Dnyaneshwari by Sant Dnyaneshwar and Gita Rahasya by Bal Gangadhar Tilak, despite their distinct approaches, converge remarkably on the central message conveyed in the Bhagavad Gita. Dnyaneshwari emphasizes the path of devotion (bhakti) intertwined with monism, advocating for selfless action and surrender to the divine will as pathways to spiritual realization and ethical living. On the other hand, Gita Rahasya interprets Karma Yoga through a nationalist lens, highlighting duty-bound ethics and ethical integrity in service to the nation. Despite these differences, both texts underscore the Bhagavad Gita's teachings on the unity of self (Atman) and the divine (Brahman), the importance of ethical conduct

(Dharma), and the pursuit of spiritual liberation through disciplined action and devotion. They collectively affirm the timeless relevance of the Gita's central message, resonating with seekers of truth across diverse philosophical, cultural, and spiritual traditions. Interpreted in different eras

Author's Notes:

I reproduce below an excerpt from the preface to the translation of 'Dnyaneshwari' by M.R. Yardi.

"The Shankara-Bhashya (Commentary on Advaita Vedanta by Adi Shankaracharya) and Dnyaneshwari also differ in their view as to which Yoga is considered more important in the Gita. Shri Shankara regards the Yoga of knowledge as primary, with both the Yoga of action and the Yoga of devotion, as subsidiary and supportive to it. He states that the seeker attains liberation in the following order - purification of the mind through karma yoga, renunciation, the way of knowledge, and self-realization. In the opinion of Shri Jnaneshwar, all the methods of Yoga are equally valid, and one has to adopt the Yoga accordingly, to his aptitude. Shri Jnaneshwar, while commenting on the Yoga of meditation in the sixth chapter, has expounded the Yoga of Kundalini and extolled it as pantharaja, the best way. He has explained this Yoga in other chapters also. This view may not have been acceptable to Shri Shankara. Further, Shri Jnaneshwar says that the performance of one's duty is tantamount to nitya-yajna, and if it is performed in a selfless spirit and with dedication to God, it leads to liberation independently. Further, he says that in order to reach the lofty peak of liberation, devotion is an easy footpath and that it is attained step by step (kramayoga) by performing one's duty, devotion to God, attainment of knowledge, and non-dual devotion. In this way, the devotee becomes jnani-bhakta, who is most dear to God, and becomes one with him. On the other

hand, the other commentators of God hold, that liberation is achieved through devotion to a personal God, and even after the attainment of liberation, the devotee retains his individuality and lives in the presence of God. It is thus obvious, that Shri Jnaneshwar consulted the Shankarabhashya and not the other commentators. But he did not follow it blindly but formed his views about the message of the Gita."

Chapter 7

Social and Political Transformations

Social and political impact of Dnyaneshwari and Gita Rahasya

Socio-political implications of literature

Literature, throughout history, has wielded considerable influence over social and political landscapes, shaping ideologies, challenging norms, and reflecting societal aspirations and anxieties. Literature serves as a mirror reflecting the social, cultural, and political ambience of its time. Writers draw from individual experiences, observations, and historical contexts to craft narratives that capture the complexities of human existence. By portraying characters, settings, and conflicts, literature offers insights into societal values, beliefs, and aspirations, providing readers with a deeper understanding of their own culture and identity.

Literary works often critique prevailing social norms and practices, challenging readers to question established beliefs and institutions. For example, novels like George Orwell's "1984" and Margaret Atwood's "The Handmaid's Tale" critique totalitarian regimes and patriarchal systems, respectively, prompting readers to reflect on issues of power, control, and individual freedom in society. Literature amplifies marginalized voices and perspectives, offering a platform for underrepresented groups to tell their stories and advocate for social justice. Works such as Toni Morrison's "Beloved" and Chimamanda Ngozi Adichie's "Half of a Yellow Sun" explore themes of race, identity, and colonialism, shedding light on experiences that challenge dominant narratives and broaden readers' empathy and understanding. Literature has historically played a crucial role in driving social movements and advocating for political reform. Writers often use their craft to inspire empathy, provoke action, and mobilize communities around issues of injustice and inequality. During the Civil Rights Movement in the United States, literary works such as Ralph Ellison's "Invisible Man" and James Baldwin's "The Fire Next Time" articulated the experiences of African Americans and challenged systemic racism. These works not only galvanized public support for civil rights but also influenced policymakers and legislators to enact meaningful change. Feminist literature, from Virginia Woolf's "A Room of One's Own" to contemporary works like Roxane Gay's "Bad Feminist," has critiqued gender inequality, advocated for women's rights, and sparked conversations about representation and inclusivity. These works have empowered women to challenge patriarchal structures and envision a more equitable society.

Literature has been instrumental in shaping and critiquing political ideologies, offering nuanced perspectives on governance, power dynamics, and the human condition. Dystopian literature, such as Aldous Huxley's "Brave New World" and Ray Bradbury's "Fahrenheit 451," explores totalitarian regimes, censorship, and the erosion of individual freedoms. These works serve as cautionary tales, urging readers to safeguard democratic values and resist authoritarianism. Literature plays a crucial role in shaping national identity and preserving cultural heritage. Works like Gabriel Garcia Marquez's "One Hundred Years of Solitude" celebrate Latin American history and traditions, while Chinua Achebe's "Things Fall Apart" explores the impact of colonialism on African societies. These narratives foster pride in cultural diversity and challenge hegemonic narratives imposed by colonial powers.

Literature's social and political implications are profound and enduring. By critiquing social norms, amplifying marginalized voices, driving social change, and shaping political ideologies, literature enriches public discourse, fosters empathy, and inspires collective action. As readers engage with diverse narratives and perspectives, literature continues to serve as a catalyst for dialogue, understanding, and transformation in societies worldwide. Its ability to reflect, challenge, and envision possibilities for a more just and equitable world underlines its enduring relevance and influence in shaping the future of humanity.

Understanding the social implications of Dnyaneshwari and Gita Rahasya

The caste (Dnyaneshwari)

In the 13th century, Maharashtra, like much of medieval India, was deeply entrenched in a caste-based social system that structured every aspect of life. This system, known as varna vyavastha, was not only a social hierarchy but also a religious and economic framework that dictated people's roles, professions, and interactions. At the top of this hierarchy were the Brahmins, priests, and scholars who held spiritual authority and were responsible for rituals and teaching. Below them were the Kshatriyas, warriors, and rulers who protected society and governed kingdoms. Vaishyas, the merchants and traders, formed the third varna, responsible for commerce and agricultural activities. At the bottom were the Shudras, laborers, and artisans who supported the functioning of society through manual labour. However, beyond these four varnas were the Dalits, or "untouchables," who were considered outside the varna system altogether. They performed menial tasks and were subjected to severe social discrimination and exclusion. This exclusion extended to basic rights such as access to education, temples, and public spaces. The caste system in 13th-century Maharashtra was not merely a social structure but deeply intertwined with religion, particularly through the concept of dharma. According to religious texts, each varna had its prescribed duties (karma) and responsibilities, which were believed to be essential for maintaining cosmic order and harmony (dharma). These duties were inherited and strictly observed, ensuring social stability but also perpetuating inequalities. The enforcement of caste-based norms was pervasive, with marriages strictly regulated within varna boundaries and occupations passed down through generations. Social interactions, dining practices, and even physical proximity were governed by caste rules, leading to segregated living patterns and restricted mobility for lower castes. Economically, caste determined access to resources and opportunities. Land ownership, for instance, was concentrated among upper castes, while lower castes often worked as tenants or laborers on their land. This economic disparity reinforced social hierarchies and limited upward mobility for those born into lower castes.

Dnyaneshwar intelligently applied teachings from the Bhagavad Gita, a sacred text, to also propagate the message of social equality. His

Dnyaneshwari can also be exclusively viewed as a commentary against the social evils of caste-based hierarchies. Dnyaneshwari critiques the caste system prevalent in medieval India, challenging the notion of social hierarchy based on birth. He argues for spiritual equality and universal brotherhood, asserting that devotion and ethical conduct are accessible to all individuals regardless of caste or social status. Dnyaneshwari's teachings encourage a society where individuals are valued for their inner qualities and spiritual dedication, promoting inclusivity and social justice. His teachings transcend caste and social distinctions, advocating for spiritual merit and ethical conduct as the true measures of human worth. By emphasizing devotion as a unifying force and rejecting the hierarchical caste system, Dnyaneshwari promotes social equality based on spiritual principles rather than social status.

Social Integration through quotidian expression (Dnyaneshwari)

In the 13th century Maharashtra, the availability and accessibility of religious texts were indeed limited to a privileged few, predominantly members of the king's court and elite Brahmin scholars. Religious texts, particularly Hindu scriptures like the Vedas, Puranas, and philosophical treatises, were primarily composed and transmitted in Sanskrit. Sanskrit was considered the language of the elites, scholars, and religious practitioners. Its complexity and exclusivity meant that only those with formal education and access to Brahminical traditions could understand and interpret these texts. Due to the exclusive nature of Sanskrit, religious texts circulated within narrow circles of Brahmin priests, scholars, and royal courts. The dissemination of knowledge was controlled and regulated, with manuscripts often preserved in royal libraries or monastic institutions under the patronage of kings and nobles. Brahmin scholars played a crucial role as custodians and interpreters of religious texts. They were responsible for performing rituals, conducting ceremonies, and imparting religious knowledge to the king and his courtiers. Their authority and status were derived from their mastery of Sanskrit texts and their ability to interpret complex religious doctrines. He restricted access to religious texts in Sanskrit and reinforced social hierarchies and divisions within society. It perpetuated the dominance of Brahminical orthodoxy and limited the religious and intellectual autonomy of lower castes and marginalized groups. It also contributed to the cultural and linguistic hegemony of Sanskrit over regional languages.

Sant Dnyaneshwar was a part of the quotidian revolution which began the use of local languages, in his case Marathi, for religious discourse and literary expression. By creating an adaptation of the Bhagavad Gita in the local Marathi language, Dnyaneshwar perhaps delivered one of the most significant outcomes of his work, Dnyaneshwari - social integration. The transformative potential of regional languages on religious and cultural practices was immense. Provincial expression facilitated broader accessibility to religious knowledge and practices among diverse social groups, leading to their integration into everyday life and local cultures.

Nationalism (Gita Rahasya)

Tilak's nationalist interpretation emphasizes the importance of social equality within the framework of national unity, promoting a cohesive society where every individual's contribution is valued and respected. His interpretation stresses the importance of selfless action (Nishkam Karma) and service to society (Rashtra Dharma), emphasizing that all individuals contribute to the welfare of the nation irrespective of their social background. By promoting a sense of collective responsibility and ethical governance, Gita Rahasya fosters social equality through a framework of moral integrity and national solidarity. Tilak's interpretation of Bhagavad Gita resonated deeply with freedom fighters who saw themselves as warriors in the struggle against the

British colonial rule. Gita Rahasya's teachings inspired them to uphold the principles laid down by Tilak, in their fight for independence, viewing their struggle as a sacred duty (dharma) for the welfare of the nation.

Tilak's intellect found a spiritual basis for nationalism. He emphasized the Gita's message of unity and harmony as essential for social welfare. He argued that India's diverse communities should come together under a common national identity, transcending caste, creed, and regionality. This message of unity provided a spiritual basis for forging a united front against colonial rule and fostering solidarity among Indians. By asserting the relevance of Indian spiritual traditions in contemporary political discourse, Tilak sought to instil pride in Indian cultural identity and heritage among nationalists. Tilak's perspective on righteous rule influenced nationalist leaders to aspire for a just and principled governance model once India achieved independence, shaping discussions on the ethical responsibilities of leadership.

Political Mileage

Tilak advocated for legal and political reforms based on principles derived from the Gita. He argued for the establishment of a just and ethical governance system (rajadharma) that prioritized the welfare of the people. Tilak's writings influenced nationalist leaders to articulate demands for constitutional reforms, self-governance, and social justice, laying the groundwork for future political movements and reforms in India. In summary, the "Gita Rahasya" by Bal Gangadhar Tilak had profound political implications by providing a spiritual and philosophical foundation for Indian nationalism, inspiring resistance against British rule, promoting cultural revivalism, challenging colonial ideologies, and advocating for political and social reforms. Tilak's interpretation of the Bhagavad Gita continues to resonate in India's collective memory as a symbol of moral courage, cultural pride, and the enduring quest for freedom and justice.

Conclusion

One of the central premises of this book is to study how literature transcends centuries by capturing universal themes and truths that resonate across time, culture, and geography. Through its narratives, prose, and poetry, literature serves as a bridge connecting past, present, and future generations. It endures because it speaks to fundamental aspects of human experience: love, loss, ambition, conflict, and resilience. By probing into the complexities of characters and societies, literature offers perspectives on historical events, societal norms, and moral dilemmas that remain relevant regardless of the era. Moreover, literature evolves as interpretations and contexts change over time. It invites reinterpretation and adaptation, ensuring its continued relevance in addressing contemporary issues and reflecting societal shifts. Through its ability to provoke empathy, spark dialogue, and challenge perspectives, literature fosters a deeper understanding of ourselves and others. It serves as a repository of cultural heritage and collective memory, preserving stories and ideas that shape identities and foster a sense of continuity across generations. In essence, literature transcends centuries by tapping into the essence of what it means to be human, forging connections between diverse cultures and epochs, and enriching our understanding of the past while guiding us toward a more enlightened future.

The legacy of ancient texts predominantly lives through their everlasting relevance in the socio-political context. Both Dnyaneshwari and Gita Rahasya advocate for social equality and justice. Dnyaneshwari, through its teachings on devotion and spiritual unity, transcends caste and social barriers, promoting inclusivity and harmony among diverse communities. Similarly, Gita Rahasya highlights the importance of ethical conduct and service to society, emphasizing the welfare of all citizens irrespective of caste or creed. By examining these scriptures, we gain a deeper understanding of the oneness between indrividual morality and societal well-being, highlighting the enduring importance of timeless wisdom in navigating the complexities of human existence. Their teachings not only had a profound influence in the times these works were given birth but also influenced one and all in subsequent generations. As we reflect on their teachings, we are reminded of the enduring relevance of ancient texts in shaping the understanding of social justice, political ethics, and the quest for a harmonious society.

The enduring socio-political relevance of ancient texts is a testament to their profound and timeless wisdom. The Dnyaneshwari and Gita Rahasya, as exemplars of this legacy, offer insights that transcend their historical contexts. They illuminate fundamental principles of governance, ethics, and social harmony that remain pertinent in today's world. By exploring these texts, we uncover invaluable lessons on leadership, justice, and the interplay between individual responsibility and collective well-being. Their legacy lies not merely in their antiquity, but in their capacity to inspire critical reflection and guide contemporary discourse on the enduring quest for a just and harmonious society. Thus, the study and interpretation of ancient texts continue to enrich the understanding of socio-political dynamics, reinforcing their relevance across generations.

Author's Notes:

Tilak's political philosophy was rooted in the concept of Swaraj or self-rule. He believed that Indians must assert their right to govern themselves and actively participate in shaping their destiny. This vision was encapsulated in his famous declaration, "Swarajya is my birthright, and I shall have it," which became a rallying cry for the nationalist movement (Bhatia, 1979). Central to Tilak's political strategy was the mobilization of the masses through grassroots activism and mass communication. He utilized his platform as a journalist and editor of newspapers like Kesari and Maratha to propagate nationalist ideas and galvanize public opinion (Koparkar, 2013). Tilak's newspapers played a crucial role in disseminating anti-colonial sentiments, promoting Indian culture and traditions, and criticizing British policies that undermined Indian interests.

Cultural revivalism was another cornerstone of Tilak's political thought. He emphasized the importance of reconnecting with India's rich cultural heritage as a means of fostering national pride and solidarity. Tilak popularized festivals like Ganesh Chaturthi as public celebrations, transforming them into occasions for the collective assertion of Indian identity and resistance against British cultural hegemony (Brown, 1993). Tilak's approach to politics was characterized by a blend of moderation and militant nationalism. He advocated for constructive engagement with British authorities while simultaneously organizing protests and civil disobedience campaigns to challenge colonial rule. His leadership in the Indian National Congress (INC) saw him advocating for Swadeshi (indigenous goods) and boycott movements to promote economic self-sufficiency and weaken British economic control (Koparkar, 2013).

Despite facing multiple imprisonments and government restrictions on his activities, Tilak remained steadfast in his commitment to India's freedom struggle until his passing in 1920. His legacy continues to inspire generations of Indians, symbolizing the resilience, determination, and intellectual rigor of the early nationalist movement.

Tilak's life and work serve as a testament to the power of ideas, leadership, and mass mobilization in challenging colonial domination and advancing the cause of freedom.

References

Bhatia, B. M. (1979). *Lokmanya Tilak: Father of Indian Unrest and Maker of Modern India*

Brown, J. S. (1993). *Ganesh: Studies of an Asian God*

Koparkar, P. V. (2013). *Lokmanya Tilak: His Social and Political Thoughts*

Chapter 8

Impact and Legacy

Shaping spiritual and intellectual discourse across generations

Literature, with its enduring and timeless impact, possesses a remarkable potential to shape and influence humanity across generations. Through its narratives, poetry, and philosophical reflections, literature transcends the boundaries of time and space, offering deep insights into the human experience and serving as a repository of cultural heritage. Literature wields its potential, examining its ability to provoke thought, foster empathy, preserve history, and inspire change. To begin with, literature serves as a powerful medium for exploring and understanding the complexities of human emotions and relationships. Whether through Shakespearean tragedies, Russian novels, or modern poetry, literature burrows into universal themes such as love, loss, betrayal, and redemption, resonating with readers of diverse backgrounds and experiences. By presenting characters and situations that mirror our struggles and triumphs, literature cultivates empathy and compassion, fostering a deeper understanding of both us and others. Importantly, Literature preserves and transmits cultural heritage and historical narratives. From ancient epics like the Mahabharata and the Odyssey to contemporary works that reflect current societal concerns, literature encapsulates the values, beliefs, and traditions of societies throughout history. It serves as a bridge between past and present, allowing readers to connect with the wisdom and experiences of previous generations while providing valuable insights into the evolution of human thought and civilization. It also challenges prevailing norms and ideologies, offering alternative perspectives and sparking critical discourse. Through dystopian fiction, satirical writings, or allegorical tales, authors critique societal injustices, political systems, and the human condition itself. By questioning established truths and presenting new possibilities, literature encourages readers to engage critically with their surroundings and envision a more just and equitable world. Further, literature inspires creativity and innovation across various art forms and disciplines. The works of poets, novelists, and playwrights have influenced painters, composers, filmmakers, and scientists, shaping cultural movements, and advancing human knowledge. The enduring legacy of literary classics such as Dante's "Divine Comedy," or Mary Shelley's "Frankenstein," illustrates how literature continues to inspire and provoke intellectual curiosity and exploration. To add, literature also offers solace and companionship in times of adversity. Through literature, individuals find refuge, guidance, and a sense of belonging, particularly during moments of personal crisis or societal upheaval. Books become lifelong companions, providing comfort, encouragement, and wisdom that resonate deeply with readers throughout their lives.

Impact and Legacy of Dnyaneshwari

Literature	Spirituality	Social	Cultural	Political	Education
• Marathi Poetry • Literary Genius	• Monism • Bhakti • Path of Devotion	• Equality • Inclusivity	• Heritage • Festivals	• Guidance • Governance	• Academic • Philosophy

Literature

Dnyaneshwari holds a revered position in Marathi literature and has had a profound impact on its development and evolution.

Pioneering Use of Provincial Language: Dnyaneshwari is significant for being one of the earliest major works in Marathi literature written in the regional language. At the time, Sanskrit was the dominant language for scholarly and religious texts, inaccessible to the common people. Dnyaneshwar's decision to write in Marathi democratized access to spiritual knowledge, making profound philosophical ideas accessible to a wider audience. This marked a significant milestone in the development of Marathi as a literary language and laid the foundation for its future growth and richness.

Literary Style and Poetic Excellence: Dnyaneshwari is celebrated for its lyrical beauty, poetic imagery, and profound philosophical insights. Sant Dnyaneshwar's poetic genius shines through his commentary, which transforms the complex teachings into accessible and engaging Marathi verse. His use of metaphor, allegory, and poetic devices captivates readers and enriches the literary experience, setting a high standard for subsequent Marathi poets and writers.

Influence on Literary Tradition: Dnyaneshwari inspired generations of poets and writers in Maharashtra and beyond. Its impact on Marathi literature can be seen in the subsequent development of Bhakti literature, which continued to explore themes of devotion, spirituality, and the human quest for divine knowledge. The commentary's fusion of spiritual teachings with literary excellence established a tradition of philosophical discourse in Marathi literature, influencing genres such as abhangas (devotional poetry) and kirtans (devotional songs).

Spirituality

The spiritual impact of Dnyaneshwari is multifaceted and profound, influencing individuals and communities in numerous ways.

Accessible Spiritual Knowledge: Dnyaneshwari made the teachings of the Bhagavad Gita accessible to the common people by translating them into Marathi. This democratization of spiritual knowledge enabled individuals from all walks of life, irrespective of their educational background or social status, to engage deeply with the profound spiritual wisdom contained in the Gita.

Integration of Bhakti and Jnana: One of the significant contributions of Dnyaneshwari is its integration of the paths of devotion (bhakti) and knowledge (jnana). It emphasizes that true spiritual realization comes from a combination of deep understanding (jnana) of spiritual truths and heartfelt devotion (bhakti) to God. This integration provided a balanced approach to spirituality that resonated with seekers looking for both intellectual clarity and emotional connection in their spiritual practice.

Emphasis on Practical Spirituality: Dnyaneshwari emphasizes the practical application of spiritual principles in daily life. It stresses the importance of performing one's duties (karma) with devotion and righteousness (dharma) while maintaining a detached attitude towards the outcomes of actions. This practical approach to spirituality resonated deeply with individuals striving to integrate their spiritual beliefs into their everyday responsibilities and interactions.

Promotion of Universal Values: Through its teachings, Dnyaneshwari promotes universal values such as compassion, tolerance, non-violence, and selflessness. It encourages individuals to cultivate virtues and qualities that lead to inner harmony and peace, fostering a sense of oneness with all beings and a deeper understanding of the underlying unity in diversity.

The catalyst for Bhakti Movement: Dnyaneshwari played a crucial role in the Bhakti movement in Maharashtra, inspiring a wave of devotion to God that transcended caste, creed, and societal divisions. It contributed to the cultural and social reformation by emphasizing personal devotion and spiritual experience over rigid ritualism and orthodoxy.

Social Reform

Promotion of Social Equality: Dnyaneshwari emphasized the universal spiritual principles of equality, compassion, and non-discrimination. It challenged prevailing social hierarchies and caste distinctions by asserting the spiritual equality of all beings. This message resonated with the Bhakti movement's ideals, promoting a more inclusive and egalitarian society where devotion to God and spiritual merit were considered more significant than social status or birth.

Ethical and Moral Guidance: The teachings of Dnyaneshwari provided ethical and moral guidance to individuals and communities.

It emphasized the importance of righteous conduct (dharma) and ethical behavior in both personal and societal contexts. This ethical framework helped promote a sense of responsibility towards others and encouraged individuals to lead virtuous lives based on spiritual principles.

Social Inclusivity: By emphasizing that devotion to God and understanding of spiritual truths are accessible to all, Dnyaneshwari promotes inclusivity in the sphere of spiritual practice and realization. Its teachings aim to inspire individuals and communities to embrace inclusivity, compassion, and spiritual growth, transcending barriers of caste, creed, and social status.

Cultural influence

Cultural Identity: Dnyaneshwari played a vital role in shaping the cultural identity of Maharashtra. It articulated spiritual teachings and philosophical insights in the language and cultural context familiar to the people of the region. Through its teachings on devotion (bhakti), knowledge (jnana), and ethical conduct (dharma), Dnyaneshwari fostered a sense of cultural pride and identity rooted in spiritual values and ethical principles.

Artistic expression: The teachings and themes of Dnyaneshwari have inspired various forms of artistic expression, including music, dance, and visual arts. Bhajan and kirtan traditions in Maharashtra often draw upon the devotional sentiments and spiritual themes articulated in Dnyaneshwari. The work continues to inspire musicians, dancers, and artists to create art that reflects its spiritual essence and cultural significance. Dnyaneshwar's use of Ovi meter has influenced generations of poets in India.

Cultural traditions: One of the most significant cultural traditions influenced by Dnyaneshwari is the Wari procession to Pandharpur, known as the Pandharpur Wari. This annual pilgrimage involves thousands of devotees (called warkaris) walking from various towns and villages in Maharashtra to the town of Pandharpur, where they visit the Vitthala temple. Dnyaneshwari's emphasis on devotion (bhakti) to Vitthala (a form of Lord Vishnu) has contributed to the popularity and spiritual significance of this pilgrimage. During the Wari, devotees sing abhangas (devotional songs) composed by saints like Dnyaneshwar, which reflect the teachings and philosophy found in Dnyaneshwari.

Abhangas and Bhajans: Dnyaneshwari's teachings have inspired the composition of numerous abhangas and bhajans (devotional songs) dedicated to Vitthala and other deities revered in Maharashtra. These devotional songs are sung during religious ceremonies, festivals, and cultural events, promoting communal singing and collective worship. The lyrical beauty and spiritual depth of Dnyaneshwari continue to resonate through these musical traditions, fostering a sense of spiritual unity and devotion among the people.

Cultural Festivals: Dnyaneshwari's influence is also evident in various cultural festivals celebrated in Maharashtra. Festivals like Ashadhi Ekadashi and Kartiki Ekadashi are dedicated to Vitthala and are observed with fasting, prayer, and devotional rituals. These festivals mark important occasions for devotees to reflect on the teachings of Dnyaneshwari, emphasizing spiritual devotion and ethical living.

Literary and Artistic Celebrations: Dnyaneshwari's impact extends to literary and artistic celebrations that honour Marathi literature and cultural heritage. Literary festivals and seminars often feature discussions on Dnyaneshwari's philosophical insights and literary contributions, highlighting its enduring relevance in contemporary discourse. Art exhibitions, dance performances, and theatrical adaptations inspired by Dnyaneshwari further enrich the cultural landscape, preserving and promoting its teachings through creative expression.

Political Influence

Dnyaneshwari may not have had direct, explicit political doctrines, however, its influence on Maharashtra's socio-religious fabric and cultural identity indirectly contributed to shaping political consciousness and fostering movements that sought social justice, equality, and cultural preservation.

Dnyaneshwari promotes a model of leadership that is rooted in ethical conduct, selfless service, wisdom, and a sense of duty toward the welfare of society. It provides a spiritual and philosophical framework for understanding governance and leadership, emphasizing the integration of spiritual values with practical governance principles. The text advocates for leaders to govern with fairness and justice, ensuring that all members of society are treated equitably. It guides leaders to uphold principles of fairness in their decisions and policies, promoting harmony and social well-being. True leadership, according to the Dnyaneshwari, involves humility and a sense of service towards others. It prescribes leaders to not be driven by ego or desire for personal glory but should serve their people with compassion and empathy. Dnyaneshwari teaches that leadership requires wisdom and knowledge. Leaders are advised to cultivate self-awareness, understanding of human nature, and discernment in decision-making. It states that wisdom comes from a deeper spiritual understanding rather than mere intellectual prowess. Leaders are expected to act ethically and responsibly, guided by a sense of duty towards their subjects and society at large.

Dnyaneshwari also imparts several governance principles that are rooted in ethical and spiritual ideals. It emphasizes the importance of governance based on dharma, which refers to righteous conduct and adherence to moral principles. The text advocates for governance that respects and promotes equality among all members of society. Leaders are encouraged to create inclusive policies that ensure the welfare and dignity of every individual, regardless of caste, creed, or socioeconomic status. Dnyaneshwari emphasizes the importance of humility and compassion in governance. Compassion towards the suffering and needs of others is seen as essential for effective governance. Dnyaneshwari calls for upholding lofty standards of integrity and accountability in governance. It requires governance to be transparent, accountable, and trustworthy to its constituents. Dnyaneshwari promotes governance that fosters harmony and social well-being and promotes social cohesion, unity, and peaceful coexistence. It states that policies and decisions should aim to enhance the overall welfare and happiness of society.

Education

Dnyaneshwari's contributions to the field of academics are significant, particularly in the domains of philosophy, literature, and spiritual studies. The Philosophical commentary in Dnyaneshwari provided scholars and thinkers with a comprehensive framework rooted in monism (Advaita Vedanta) and devotion (Bhakti traditions). Dnyaneshwari's exploration and exposition of Bhagavad Gita has enriched philosophical discourse in Indian academia, influencing subsequent generations of philosophers, scholars, and thinkers. The richness of discourse in Dnyaneshwari inspired many, through generations, with a result of renewed interest to follow in theological studies.

Dnyaneshwari's accessible explanation of complex philosophical concepts made spiritual teachings more approachable to a wider audience. It became a foundational text in the curriculum of traditional Indian education systems, including Gurukuls and Pathshalas, where it continues to be studied for its educational value and moral teachings. Its pedagogical impact lies in its ability to convey profound spiritual truths through storytelling and allegory, facilitating deeper understanding and reflection among students and scholars alike. Dnyaneshwari's impact transcended its immediate socio-religious context to influence the establishment of educational institutions dedicated to the study of Marathi literature, philosophy, and spirituality. These institutions played a crucial role in disseminating knowledge and fostering intellectual growth among students interested in the teachings of Dnyaneshwar and other Bhakti saints.

Finally, Dnyaneshwari's impact on education can be seen in its promotion of the Marathi language, revival of the Bhakti tradition, influence on philosophical thought, contribution to cultural identity, and establishment of educational institutions. Its legacy continues to inspire educational endeavours that celebrate linguistic diversity, promote spiritual inquiry, and enrich intellectual discourse in Maharashtra and beyond.

Impact and Legacy of Gita Rahasya

Like Dnyaneshwari, has had a multifaceted impact on philosophy, politics, culture, education, and literature, and continues to be relevant in contemporary discussions.

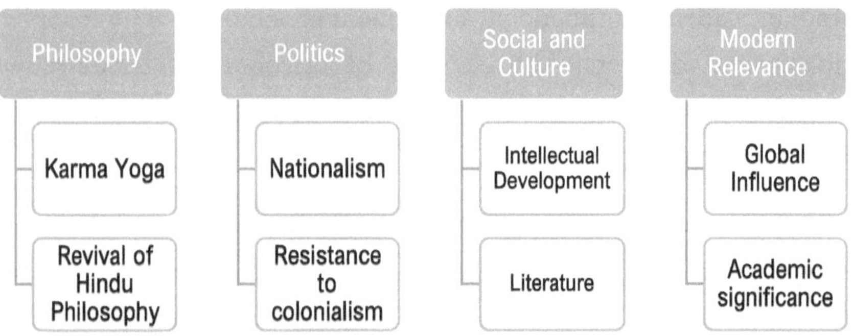

Impact of Tilak's Philosophy in Gita Rahasya

Tilak's interpretation of the Bhagavad Gita, presented in Gita Rahasya dives deep into the philosophical underpinnings of Hindu thought and has influenced several aspects of philosophical discourse. His perspective on Karma Yoga has resonated widely in philosophical circles by presenting a practical approach to spirituality that integrates daily actions with higher spiritual ideas. Gita Rahasya's philosophical stance on righteous duty has influenced discussions on ethics and moral philosophy highlighting the significance of ethical conduct which is projected as a cornerstone of Hindu philosophy. Integration of Advaita Vedanta (monism) with Bhakti traditions (devotion) and Karma Yoga (action) has enriched philosophical debates on the nature of reality, self, and the divine. This has also helped foster a deeper understanding of the philosophical depth and universality of the original sacred text – Bhagavad Gita. Tilak's interpretation of Karma Yoga as a call for action towards the upliftment of society added a whole new dimension to its popular philosophical construct. Gita Rahasya remains a cornerstone in the study of the Bhagavad Gita and continues to inspire philosophical discussions on karma, dharma, self-realization, and the pursuit of spiritual enlightenment.

Political Influence of Gita Rahasya

Gita Rahasya is not only a profound philosophical treatise but also a work that had a significant political impact and influence during the Indian independence movement.

Nationalism: Tilak's interpretation of the Bhagavad Gita in "Gita Rahasya" inspired a sense of nationalism among Indians. He interpreted the Gita's teachings on duty (dharma) and action (karma) as a call to duty towards the nation. Tilak, through his Gita Rahasya, encouraged Indians to rise against colonial rule and asserted that the struggle for independence was not just a political movement but also a righteous duty (karma yoga) towards the motherland.

The resurgence of Hindu Identity: "Gita Rahasya" played a role in reviving and asserting Hindu cultural and religious identity during a time of colonial domination. Tilak's interpretation emphasized the relevance of ancient Hindu scriptures in modern times and reaffirmed the spiritual and moral foundations of Hindu society. This resurgence of Hindu identity was politically significant as it galvanized support for the independence movement among Hindus who saw it as a struggle to preserve their cultural and religious heritage.

Mobilisation and Resistance: Tilak used "Gita Rahasya" as a tool for mobilizing the masses against British colonialism. His interpretation of the Gita's teachings on righteous action and selfless service inspired Indians to participate actively in the freedom struggle. The work contributed to the mobilization of people across different regions and communities, uniting them under a common cause of national liberation.

Change to Colonial Narratives: Tilak's scholarly approach demonstrated the depth and sophistication of Hindu thought, countering colonial stereotypes and misrepresentations. This challenge to colonial narratives helped foster a sense of pride in Indian cultural and intellectual heritage, laying the groundwork for a renewed assertion of Indian identity and independence.

Social & Cultural Reforms

Gita Rahasya had a social and cultural impact on the fabric of Indian society.

Revival of Cultural Identity: Tilak's interpretation of the Bhagavad Gita in "Gita Rahasya" played a crucial role in reviving and reaffirming India's cultural identity again in the 20th century. This revival of cultural identity was instrumental in fostering a sense of pride and unity among Indians, particularly during a period of colonial dominance that sought to undermine Indigenous traditions and values.

Essence of Hindu spirituality: The work influenced religious discourse by emphasizing the universal and timeless relevance of Gita's teachings, transcending sectarian divides, and promoting a holistic understanding of Hindu spirituality. Situated in a period just a few decades before the Indian freedom struggle gathered pace and before the actual independence, the perspective shaped by Gita Rahasya was immensely valuable.

Cultural renaissance: The social impact of "Gita Rahasya" extended beyond scholarly circles to inspire a cultural renaissance. The work played a vital role in mobilizing the masses for social reform, educational empowerment, and political activism, laying the groundwork for India's independence movement and nation-building efforts. Its legacy continues to resonate in India's socio-cultural fabric, contributing to the preservation and celebration of its rich cultural heritage and spiritual traditions.

Modern Relevance

Tilak's interpretation of the Bhagavad Gita in "Gita Rahasya" presents a profound philosophical perspective that transcends cultural boundaries.

Philosophical relevance: His exposition on karma yoga (path of selfless action), dharma (duty/righteousness), and the nature of the self has resonated with philosophers and spiritual seekers worldwide. The universal themes and ethical principles discussed in "Gita Rahasya" appeal to individuals seeking deeper insights into human existence, morality, and spirituality beyond specific religious affiliations.

Interfaith dialogue and understanding: The teachings and interpretations presented in "Gita Rahasya" have facilitated interfaith dialogue and understanding. By emphasizing universal spiritual truths and the unity of all beings, Tilak's work promotes harmony and mutual respect among different religious and cultural traditions. Scholars and practitioners from diverse backgrounds have studied "Gita Rahasya" to gain insights into Hindu philosophy and its implications for broader theological and ethical discussions.

Comparative religion studies: "Gita Rahasya" has contributed to comparative religion studies by providing a comprehensive exploration of Hindu philosophy within the context of global spiritual traditions. Its insights into karma, dharma, and the pursuit of spiritual liberation offer valuable perspectives for understanding similarities and differences across religious doctrines. The work serves as a reference for scholars examining the intersection of Eastern and Western philosophies, enriching academic discourse on spirituality, ethics, and the human condition.

The enduring relevance

As we reflect on the legacy of Dnyaneshwari and Gita Rahasya, we recognize their enduring relevance in today's interconnected world. These works remind us of the transformative power of spiritual wisdom, the richness of cultural heritage, and the importance of ethical leadership. They serve as guiding beacons, encouraging us to explore deeper truths, embrace diversity, and strive for collective well-being. Both, Dnyaneshwari, and Gita Rahasya stand as luminous milestones in the evolution of human thought and spiritual understanding. Their legacies endure as pillars of transcendental wisdom, philosophical inquiry, cultural pride, and educational enlightenment. These two remarkable works continue to inspire, educate, and empower individuals across generations, reaffirming their timeless significance in the pursuit of truth, righteousness, and spiritual fulfilment.

Author's Notes:

Global efforts for interfaith dialogue and understanding have become increasingly prevalent as societies navigate cultural diversity and religious pluralism. Initiatives such as the Parliament of the World's Religions serve as pivotal platforms for fostering dialogue among different faith traditions and promoting mutual respect and cooperation (Parliament of the World's Religions, n.d.). These gatherings bring together religious leaders, scholars, and activists from around the globe to discuss shared values and address pressing global issues from diverse spiritual perspectives.

Moreover, interfaith organizations like the Interfaith Youth Core (IFYC) focus on engaging young people in meaningful dialogue across religious boundaries, emphasizing the role of youth in building bridges of understanding and cooperation (Interfaith Youth Core, n.d.). IFYC's programs encourage interfaith service projects, leadership development, and educational initiatives that highlight common values while respecting religious differences.

On an international level, the United Nations promotes interfaith dialogue through various initiatives aimed at fostering peace, sustainable development, and human rights. The UN Alliance of Civilizations works to reduce tensions and promote reconciliation between diverse cultures and religions, recognizing the importance of interfaith dialogue in achieving global stability and harmony (United Nations Alliance of Civilizations, n.d.).

These global efforts underscore the transformative power of dialogue in bridging cultural divides, promoting social cohesion, and advancing shared goals of peace and justice. By nurturing understanding and cooperation among diverse religious communities, these initiatives contribute to a more inclusive and harmonious global society.

References

Interfaith Youth Core, https://www.ifyc.org/

Parliament of the World's Religions, https://www.parliamentofreligions.org/

United Nations Alliance of Civilizations, https://www.unaoc.org/

Chapter 9

Insights From Other Indian and Global Perspectives

Cross-Cultural Readings of the Bhagavad Gita: Indian and World Views

"The Bhagavad Gita is the most beautiful philosophical song existing in any known tongue"

– J. Robert Oppenheimer
(American Physicist and the Director of the Manhattan Project)

Indian culture, characterized by its remarkable receptiveness, has consistently absorbed, and synthesized a myriad of influences, creating a lush mosaic that reflects the interplay of tradition and innovation throughout history. The receptiveness of Indian culture and tradition is exemplified by its ability to accommodate a wide spectrum of beliefs, including atheistic views, reflecting a profound openness that allows for the coexistence of spiritual and secular philosophies in the pursuit of understanding and meaning. The accretion of the Bhagavad Gita over generations reflects the profound receptiveness of Indian culture to diverse ideas and philosophies. This enduring tradition demonstrates how successive generations have not only preserved these texts but also enriched them with contemporary interpretations and insights. As the Gita's teachings have been recontextualized to address the evolving social, political, and spiritual landscapes, they embody a dynamic dialogue between tradition and modernity. This willingness to embrace and adapt wisdom from various sources accentuates the flexibility and inclusivity of Indian thought, highlighting its capacity to resonate across time and space. The interpretations of the Bhagavad Gita vary widely among scholars, philosophers, and spiritual leaders both within India and around the world. Each interpreter brings a unique perspective, influenced by cultural, philosophical, and religious backgrounds. Indian authors such as Swami Vivekananda, A.C. Bhaktivedanta Swami Prabhupada, and Sri Aurobindo offer profound insights rooted in Hindu spiritual traditions. Their interpretations emphasize Gita's teachings on dharma (duty/righteousness), karma (action), and yoga (spiritual discipline), highlighting its relevance to both individual spiritual growth and societal harmony. Outside India, scholars and thinkers from diverse cultural backgrounds have also offered their interpretations of the Bhagavad Gita, often integrating its teachings with their philosophical traditions. For instance, German philosopher Arthur Schopenhauer was deeply influenced by Hindu philosophy, particularly the Upanishads and the Bhagavad Gita. He saw in the Gita a profound exposition of ethical duty and the nature of the self, which resonated with his ideas on the will and morality. These interpretations reflect the Gita's versatility and ability to inspire diverse perspectives on spiritual life, morality, and the nature of reality. Whether viewed through the lens of Hindu devotionalism, philosophical inquiry or as a practical guide for ethical living, the Bhagavad Gita continues to resonate with readers worldwide, offering timeless wisdom and guidance on the journey of self-discovery and spiritual awakening. As we explore these varied interpretations, we gain a deeper appreciation for Gita's enduring significance and its capacity to illuminate the paths to spiritual fulfilment in an ever-changing world.

Based on my limited reading of these various interpretations I have tried to tabularise these for ease of understanding. Beware, these are mere outlines of the core essence of some remarkable commentaries on the Bhagavad Gita and do not claim to be comprehensive in scope.

Indian Authors Table 9.1

Author	Key Focus	Unique Aspect	Major Work(s)
Swami Vivekananda	Karma Yoga; duty and action without attachment	Emphasis on practical application of Gita teachings in daily life	Lectures and writings on Bhagavad Gita
Mahatma Gandhi	Non-Violence; truth	Integration of Gita's teachings with principles of non-violent resistance	"Anasakti Yoga"

Author	Key Focus	Unique Aspect	Major Work(s)
Adi Shankaracharya	Advaita Vedanta, brahman, and Atman, Maya, and illusion, the path of knowledge, detachment, and renunciation, and unity of existence	Identity of the individual soul (Atman) with Brahman, discusses Maya (illusion) as the cause of ignorance and bondage, emphasizing discrimination between the eternal and ephemeral, stresses detachment, emphasizes the underlying unity of all existence, where diversity is an expression of the unity of Brahman.	Commentaries on the Bhagavad Gita, particularly his extensive commentary known as "Bhagavad Gita Bhashya", Atma Bodha, Maya Panchakam, Upadesa Sahasri, Aparoshanubhuti
A.C. Bhaktivedanta Swami Prabhupada	Bhakti Yoga	Devotional approach to Krishna as the Supreme Personality of Godhead	Bhagavad Gita As It Is
Sri Aurobindo	Integral Yoga	Evolution of consciousness and divine manifestation in human life	Essays on the Gita, Savitri
Swami Sivananda	Devotion, Action, Knowledge; Synthesis of Yoga Paths	Integration of various yoga paths (Karma, Bhakti, Raja, Jnana)	Commentary on Bhagavad Gita
Paramahansa Yogananda	Kriya Yoga	Detailed metaphysical and practical commentary	Autobiography of a Yogi, God Talks With Arjuna

Author	Key Focus	Unique Aspect	Major Work(s)
Sri Ramakrishna	Devotion and Surrender	Emphasis on direct experience of God and devotion	Teachings and Discussions
Acharya Vinoba Bhave	Spirituality, social justice, and self-realization	Emphasis on non-violence and selflessness, application & integration of Gita's teachings into daily life	Talks on the Gita (Gita Pravachane), Sarvodaya and Bhoodan Movement

Western Authors – Table 9.2

Author	Country	Key Focus	Unique Aspect	Major Work
Eknath Easwaran	USA	Yoga of Devotion (Bhakti Yoga)	Practical application, meditation	The Bhagavad Gita: A New Translation
Juan Mascaro	UK (Spain)	Spiritual Wisdom	Poetic translation, scholarly approach	The Bhagavad Gita
Christopher Isherwood	UK (USA)	Philosophical Inquiry	Modern language, philosophical commentary	The Bhagavad Gita According to Gandhi
Ralph Waldo Emerson	USA	Transcendentalism	Universal spirituality, individual interpretation	Essays and Lectures on Indian Philosophy
Annie Besant	UK	Theosophical Interpretation	Spiritual evolution, universal brotherhood	The Bhagavad Gita: A Theosophical Interpretation

Author	Country	Key Focus	Unique Aspect	Major Work
J. Robert Oppenheimer	USA	Scientific Inquiry	Modern context, philosophical reflection	-
Aldous Huxley	UK	Universal relevance	Gita's relevance to Western thought	Introduction to the Bhagavad Gita
Franklin Edgerton	USA	Scholarly and literal translation	Detailed academic translation	The Bhagavad Gita: Translated and Explained
Barbara Stoler Miller	USA	Literary and Cultural Interpretation	Poetic and accessible translation	The Bhagavad Gita: Krishna's counsel in time of war
Stephen Mitchell	USA	Literary and poetic rendering	Contemporary version	Bhagavad Gita: A New Translation
Winthrop Sargeant	USA	Comprehensive translation	Word-for-word translation with commentary	The Bhagavad Gita
Georg Feuerstein	Germany	Yogic philosophy	Broader context of Yoga	The Essence of Bhagavad Gita

Tables 9.1 and 9.2 are illustrative lists of some of the key works on Bhagavad Gita by Indian and non-Indian authors that depict a variety of interpretations.

Comparative Analysis of Indian Interpretations of the Bhagavad Gita

Interpretations of the Bhagavad Gita by Indian scholars, philosophers, and spiritual leaders can be classified and described based on several key criteria, including philosophical orientation, spiritual emphasis, practical application, and historical context. Here is an attempt to undertake a structured approach to classify and describe these interpretations.

Philosophical Orientation

Vedantic Interpretations: Advaita Vedanta emphasizes monism or non-dualism, seeing the individual soul (Atman) as identical to Brahman, the ultimate reality. Scholars like Adi Shankaracharya interpret the Gita to emphasize the unity of all existence and the realization of one's true nature. Vishishtadvaita Vedanta propounds qualified non-dualism, where the individual soul retains its identity but is also united with the universal soul. Ramanuja and other Vaishnavite scholars interpret the Gita to highlight devotion (bhakti) and service (karma) as paths to spiritual realization. Dvaita Vedanta advocates dualism, asserting the eternal distinction between the individual soul and the supreme soul. Madhvacharya and others interpret the Gita to emphasize devotion (bhakti) to a personal deity (Ishta Devata) as the means to liberation.

Yoga Philosophies: Karma Yoga focuses on selfless action and performing one's duty without attachment to outcomes. Swami Vivekananda and others interpret the Gita to emphasize the importance of righteous action and its role in spiritual growth. Jnana Yoga emphasizes knowledge and self-inquiry as paths to realization. Scholars like Swami Chinmayananda interpret the Gita to highlight the intellect's role in discerning the eternal from the temporary and realizing the self. Bhakti Yoga centres on devotion and love for the divine. Swami Sivananda and other bhakti-oriented scholars interpret the Gita to emphasize surrender to God, unconditional love, and the path of devotion as a means to liberation.

Spiritual Emphasis

Theistic perspectives: Vaishnavite Interpretations focus on devotion to Vishnu/Krishna as the supreme deity. Scholars like A.C. Bhaktivedanta Swami Prabhupada interpret the Gita through the lens of devotion (bhakti), highlighting Krishna's divine nature and teachings. Shaivite Interpretations centre on devotion to Shiva as the supreme deity. Some interpretations focus on the Gita's teachings that align with Shaiva philosophy, emphasizing the path of renunciation and devotion.

Non-Theistic perspectives: Advaita Vedanta Interpretations emphasize the non-dual nature of reality and the unity of all existence. Scholars like Swami Vivekananda interpret the Gita to emphasize the self-realization of one's true nature beyond individual identity. Universalist Interpretations focus on the Gita's universal teachings applicable to all spiritual seekers, regardless of religious affiliation or specific deity worship.

Practical applications

Social and Ethical perspectives: Karma Yoga is interpreted to emphasize the importance of ethical conduct and fulfilling one's duties selflessly. Scholars like Mahatma Gandhi and Swami Vivekananda interpret the Gita to promote social responsibility and service to humanity. Dharma and Justice interpretations focus on the Gita's teachings related to righteousness (dharma) and the ethical principles governing personal and societal conduct.

Personal Transformation: Inner Journey emphasizes the Gita's teachings as a guide for personal growth, self-discovery, and spiritual evolution. Interpretations by Sri Aurobindo and Jiddu Krishnamurti highlight the Gita's relevance in the context of individual transformation and self-realization.

Historical and Cultural Context

Revivalist Interpretations: Scholars and leaders during India's independence movement and the Hindu revival period, such as Swami Vivekananda, interpreted the Gita to inspire national pride, social reform, and spiritual awakening. Their interpretations often emphasized the Gita's relevance in modern times and its potential to guide India through socio-political challenges.

Scholarly Interpretations: Contemporary scholars and spiritual leaders interpret the Gita in light of global issues, interfaith dialogue, and universal human values. Their interpretations often focus on the Gita's message of unity, harmony, and spiritual liberation applicable to all humanity.

The interpretations of the Bhagavad Gita by Indian authors are diverse and multifaceted, reflecting the richness of Hindu philosophy and spiritual traditions. Each interpretation offers unique insights into the Gita's teachings, guiding readers on paths to spiritual realization, ethical living, and personal growth. Together, they form a colorful panorama of wisdom that continues to inspire and enlighten seekers worldwide.

Indian and Western approach to the interpretation of Bhagavad Gita

Western Approaches

Western interpretations often approach the Gita from academic and philosophical perspectives, analysing its teachings in the context of broader religious and philosophical traditions. There is a tendency to compare Gita's teachings with other religious texts and philosophical systems, seeking parallels and differences in concepts such as duty, ethics, and the nature of reality. Some Western interpretations focus on the Gita's relevance to personal growth, psychological well-being, and existential questions in contemporary life. Emphasis is placed on universal themes in the Gita, such as the nature of the self, ethical behavior, and the pursuit of inner peace, which resonate beyond religious boundaries. Western interpretations often explore how the Gita's teachings can be applied in modern contexts, such as leadership, management, and mindfulness practices. The Gita inspires artistic and literary interpretations in Western cultures, reflecting its universal appeal and adaptability across different creative mediums.

Major distinctions in Indian and non-Indian approach

The difference in approach to the interpretation of the Bhagavad Gita between Indian and Western authors can be attributed to several factors rooted in historical, cultural, philosophical, and academic contexts.

Indian authors often interpret the Bhagavad Gita within the broader context of Hindu cultural and religious traditions. They are familiar with the mythological narratives, philosophical frameworks (like Vedanta and Yoga), and religious practices that surround the text. Many Indian interpretations emphasize devotion (bhakti) to Krishna or other deities as a central aspect of spiritual practice. This devotion shapes their understanding of the Gita's teachings on love, surrender, and divine grace. Western authors approach the Bhagavad Gita from diverse cultural backgrounds, which may not have the same familiarity with Hindu mythology or religious practices. This can lead to interpretations that focus more on philosophical inquiry and comparative analysis. Western interpretations often seek to uncover universal themes in the Gita that resonate across different religious and cultural contexts. They may emphasize ethical principles, existential questions, and psychological insights that appeal beyond religious boundaries.

Indian interpretations frequently draw upon Vedantic philosophies (Advaita, Vishishtadvaita, Dvaita) and yogic paths (Karma Yoga, Bhakti Yoga, Jnana Yoga) to interpret the Gita's teachings. These philosophical frameworks provide a comprehensive lens through which to understand concepts like the nature of the self, the ultimate reality (Brahman), and the paths to spiritual liberation. Indian interpretations often emphasize the practical application of the Gita's teachings in everyday life, focusing on moral conduct, duty (dharma), and the cultivation of virtues like selflessness and compassion. Western interpretations may approach the Bhagavad Gita as a subject of academic study, exploring its teachings in comparison with other religious texts and philosophical systems. This scholarly approach often highlights similarities and differences in concepts such as ethics, metaphysics, and spirituality. Some Western interpretations study the psychological dimensions of the Gita, examining its relevance to personal growth, emotional well-being, and existential questions about the nature of life and death.

Indian interpretations often carry the weight of centuries-old commentarial traditions, influenced by revered figures like Adi Shankaracharya, Ramanuja, and Madhvacharya. These historical interpretations shape contemporary understandings of the Gita within Indian intellectual discourse. The continuity of religious and spiritual practices within India provides a living context for interpreting the Gita, where rituals, festivals, and cultural norms reinforce its teachings. Western interpretations of the Bhagavad Gita may reflect a modern academic interest in Eastern philosophy and spirituality. This approach is influenced by Western philosophical traditions, secular ethics, and the integration of Eastern thought into global philosophical discourse. The interpretation of the Gita by Western authors often fosters cross-cultural dialogue and understanding, enriching global perspectives on spirituality and ethics.

The above analysis can be summarised as follows:

Indian interpretations often explore the cultural, mythological, and religious context of the Gita, while Western interpretations may approach it from a more comparative and philosophical standpoint.

Indian interpretations frequently emphasize devotion (bhakti) and personal relationship with the divine, whereas Western interpretations may prioritize philosophical inquiry and comparative analysis.

Indian interpretations emphasize the practical application of Gita's teachings in everyday life, while Western interpretations often focus on academic study, psychological insights, and secular applications.

The difference in approach to the interpretation of the Bhagavad Gita between Indian and Western authors stems from diverse cultural backgrounds, philosophical orientations, and historical contexts. Indian interpretations are deeply rooted in traditional religious practices, philosophical frameworks, and devotional traditions, whereas Western interpretations often emphasize academic inquiry, comparative analysis, and universal themes. Both perspectives contribute to a nuanced understanding of the Gita's teachings, demonstrating its timeless relevance and universal appeal across cultures.

Epilogue

I am deeply influenced by the version composed by Acharya Vinoba Bhave. That it was my first exposure to Bhagavad Gita might have been the primary reason for this influence. "Gitai," authored by Vinoba Bhave, stands out for its minimalist and sincere approach that resonated deeply. Acharya's commentary on the Bhagavad Gita is distinguished by its simplicity and accessibility. His genuine sincerity and humane approach infuse the text with a compassionate perspective that transcends mere scholarly interpretation. Through "Gitai," Bhave not only reveals the

Gita's timeless wisdom but also integrates its teachings with practical guidance for ethical living and social responsibility. This blend of philosophical depth and simple and practical discourse has made "Gitai" a timeless source of inspiration, offering a pathway to inner peace, moral clarity, and a deeper connection with spiritual truths.

Author's Notes:

Cross-cultural interpretations of literature enrich the understanding by presenting diverse perspectives and reflecting the complexities of different societies. When readers engage with texts from cultures other than their own, they gain insights into unfamiliar customs, values, and historical contexts, broadening their worldview. For example, Gabriel Garcia Marquez's "One Hundred Years of Solitude" blends magical realism with Colombian history, offering a collage of Latin American culture that resonates globally (Marquez, 1967). The novel not only captures the cyclical nature of history but also addresses universal themes of love, family, and power, albeit through a distinctly Latin American lens. Similarly, Chinua Achebe's "Things Fall Apart" portrays the clash between traditional Igbo culture and colonialism in Nigeria, challenging readers to reconsider their assumptions about cultural superiority and the consequences of imperialism (Achebe, 1958). These works demonstrate how literature serves as a conduit for cross-cultural dialogue and understanding. Through nuanced characters and intricate plots, authors weave narratives that transcend geographical boundaries, inviting readers to empathize with experiences that may initially seem Western. By engaging with such texts, readers not only appreciate the richness of diverse cultural heritages but also confront universal truths about human nature and societal dynamics. 7

Therefore, cross-cultural interpretations of literature foster empathy, broaden perspectives, and deepen appreciation for the complexities of our interconnected world. They remind us that while cultures may differ, the human experience is fundamentally shared across time and place.

References

Achebe. C., *Things Fall Apart, 1958*, Marquez. G. G. *One Hundred Years of Solitude, 1967*

Contemporary Reflections – Perspectives for the Modern World

Unveiling contemporary wisdom from the subtle themes of Dnyaneshwari and Gita Rahasya

If a man is not actuated by the desire to acquire the knowledge of a particular science, he is unfit to study that science, and explaining such a science to such an unfit person is like pouring water on an obverse vessel. Not only is the disciple not benefited by it, but even the preceptor wastes his labour, and both waste their time.

– Lokmanya Tilak, Gita Rahasya, Ch. 3

To explore the intersection of ancient wisdom and contemporary challenges can be a profitable venture that offers valuable insights for the modern world. Much like renewable energy sources such as the sun and wind, ancient scriptures are a perennial source of wisdom for humanity. Application of teachings from the Bhagavad Gita or its interpretations such as Dnyaneshwari or Gita Rahasya has been a topic that is explored and discussed extensively by scholars, spiritual gurus, and religious leaders alike. Much has been said about how to apply the teachings from these rich texts to guide and enrich modern-day lives. I believe that the application of teachings from the Gita or from any other similar source at an individual level is best achieved through the individual's reading and comprehension of these texts, albeit with some guidance with a credible translation to the language of one's choice. As Dnyaneshwari says in Chapter one verse fifty-eight

हें शब्देंवीण संवादिजे । इंद्रियां नेणतां भोगिजे ।
बोलाआधि झोंबिजे । प्रमेयासी ॥ ५८ ॥

(It should be pondered over silently, absorbed not through the senses, and its subtle truths be grasped by the inner self even before the words meet the ears)

To adopt the teachings directly on the basis of advice from scholars and leaders, without reading the original work is neither achievable nor sustainable. This is certainly not said with an intent to undermine the expertise of the scholars and leaders but to underline the importance of self-analysis and human intellect. I certainly do not consider myself qualified enough and also do not endeavour to indulge in such an enterprise of guiding personal behaviours through this chapter. The central idea behind the inclusion of this chapter is to explore if there can be an application of certain themes from these two remarkable texts to address some of the macro-level socio-economic-political challenges that the world of today is faced with. I confess, upfront, that parts of this chapter that attempt to explore principles from these two texts to comment on the world situation may appear naïve or rhetorical. Nonetheless, I endeavour to put the black on the white to revive the awareness on some of the principles laid down by these two thought leaders.

Sanctity of age-old wisdom

तरी संभावने जिये । जो मानाची वाट पाहे ।
सत्कारें होये । तोषु जया ॥ (Dnyaneshwari Ch 13 Verse 657)
गर्वें पर्वताचीं शिखरें । तैसा महत्त्वावरूनि नुतरे ।
तयाचिया ठायीं पुरे । अज्ञान आहे ॥ (Dnyaneshwari Ch 13 Verse 658)

(If a person lives only for repute, longs for honour, and becomes overjoyed if he is treated with respect and out of pride never climbs down from his exalted position like a mountain peak, ignorance dwells in him.)

Believing in the value of teachings from ancient literature and drawing influence from them can offer profound insights and guidance. It can be justifiably assumed that the indestructible and sacred qualities attached to revered ancient wisdom that gets transitioned from one generation to the other have an inherent value, merit, and sanctity. Ancient literature often encapsulates wisdom distilled from centuries of human experience and contemplation. These teachings should presumed to have withstood the test of time, resonating across generations and cultures. They offer timeless principles and ethical guidelines that remain relevant for longer durations of time. It should also be appreciated that despite the passage of time and cultural differences, the fundamental aspects of human nature and experience remain consistent. Universal themes addressed by ancient texts are potent enough to provide insights and guidance to subsequent generations. Ethical frameworks and moral principles contained in revered ancient literature are often enduring and can be believed to be relevant across eras. The teachings on virtues like compassion, honesty, humility, and respect are a compass for ethical behaviour and responsible citizenship even today.

Finally, believing in the sanctity of teachings from ancient literature is not about blind adherence or rigid dogma but about recognizing their enduring relevance and potential to enrich contemporary life. By engaging with these teachings with an open mind and critical inquiry, valuable lessons can be learned, understanding of the world can be deepened, and society's collective wisdom and progress can be accelerated. It will certainly be worthwhile to pursue the advocacy of ancient scriptures as sources of constructive inspiration to the modern-day world. There is clearly a need to revive and relook at the teachings of Dnyaneshwari and Gita Rahasya through a lens of present-day challenges.

Without being prescriptive or advisory, let us unbiasedly analyse some of the core guiding principles laid down by the two texts which can (or should) influence the thinking of modern-day leaders and citizens. Core ideas proposed by the Dnyaneshwari, Ahimsa (non-violence), Dharma (righteousness), Nishkam Karma (selflessness), Vasudhaiva Kutumbakam (universal brotherhood), Vairagya (detachment) can be credible sources of wisdom for one and all.

Ancient wisdom is versatile

Fundamental concepts often possess a versatility that allows them to transcend specific contexts, finding application across diverse fields and situations. These concepts serve as foundational principles that can be adapted and utilized in various ways, depending on the circumstances and objectives at hand. For instance, principles like balance, ethics, and resilience have applications ranging from physics and engineering to psychology, business management, and personal development. This adaptability accentuates their enduring relevance and utility, offering frameworks for understanding, problem-solving, and decision-making across different domains of knowledge and practice.

Bhagavad Gita, Dnyaneshwari, Gita Rahasya, and similar other revered religious texts across diverse religions offer enlightenment on universal truths and fundamental virtues which will inevitably have multiple applications. For example, the concept of Dharma is relevant not only in personal ethics but also finds its application across fields of leadership, politics, governance, and professional conduct. It may therefore be worthwhile to keep going back to these fundamental virtues to find our answers. During the course of this chapter, we will keep exploring these fundamental virtues and examine their applications across multiple modern-day challenges.

Geopolitical Conflicts

जे खळांची व्यंकटी सांडो । तयां सत्कर्मीं रती वाढो ।
भूतां परस्परें पडो । मैत्र जीवाचें ॥ (Dnyaneshwari Ch 18 Verse 1795)
दुरिताचें तिमिर जावो । विश्व स्वधर्मसूर्यें पाहो ।
जो जें वांछील तो तें लाहो । प्राणिजात (Dnyaneshwari Ch 18 Verse 1796)

(May the evil shed their deviousness; May they develop a liking for virtuous deeds; May all individuals develop a spirit of fraternity; May the universe lose its sinful darkness; May the dawn of righteous duties descend; May the desires of all creatures be fulfilled.)

The landscape

In the contemporary global scenario, a multitude of geopolitical challenges shape the landscape and define the relations between nations, impacting stability, security, and prosperity on a global scale. One of the prime challenges is the resurgence of great power competition, characterized by the complex interplay between the United States, China, and Russia. This competition spans various domains, including economic influence, technological advancement, military capabilities, and ideological narratives. The United States, desperate to maintain its position as the dominant global power, faces increasing assertiveness from China, which aims to expand its sphere of influence. Russia, under Vladimir Putin's leadership, employs hybrid warfare tactics and energy diplomacy to assert influence in Eastern Europe, the Middle East, and beyond, challenging Western-led alliances and norms of international behavior.

The proliferation of non-state actors also poses significant challenges to geopolitical stability. Transnational terrorist organizations like ISIS and Al-Qaeda continue to pose threats to regional security, despite significant setbacks in recent years. Regional conflicts like those in Syria, Yemen, Palestine, and many more, each with its dynamic causes are pregnant with serious implications for global stability and humanitarian concerns. These conflicts exploit political vacuums, weak governance structures, and sectarian tensions to perpetrate violence and destabilize regions, creating ripple effects that extend far beyond their immediate operational areas. Moreover, the rise of cyber warfare capabilities among state and non-state actors introduces new dimensions of conflict, with attacks ranging from espionage and disruption of critical infrastructure to influence operations aimed at manipulating public opinion and electoral processes. The rapid evolution and diffusion of technology amplify these threats, presenting novel challenges for international norms and governance frameworks designed for a pre-digital era.

Environmental degradation and climate change exacerbate existing geopolitical tensions, particularly in resource-constrained regions. Competition over access to water, arable land, and energy resources intensifies as populations grow and climate-induced disruptions become more frequent and severe. These environmental stressors not only exacerbate humanitarian crises but also fuel conflicts over scarce resources, heightening instability and complicating efforts at conflict resolution and sustainable development.

The erosion of international norms and institutions designed to uphold global stability poses a profound challenge to the international order. The rise of populism, nationalism, and authoritarianism in various parts of the world undermines multilateral cooperation and collective security mechanisms, leading to unilateral actions, protectionist policies, and a decline in trust and cooperation among nations. The weakening of institutions such as the United Nations and the World Trade Organization undermines their ability to address global challenges effectively, leaving gaps that are often exploited by state and non-state actors pursuing narrow self-interests.

Humanitarian crises and mass displacement also strain global stability and exacerbate regional conflicts. The Syrian civil war, for example, has led to millions of refugees seeking safety in neighbouring countries and beyond, placing immense strain on host communities and contributing to political tensions in Europe and beyond. The Rohingya crisis in Myanmar, the ongoing conflict in Yemen, and the humanitarian situation in Venezuela are among the many examples of crises with profound geopolitical implications, including regional destabilization, the spread of extremism, and challenges to international humanitarian norms and obligations.

Themes adopted by Dnyaneshwari and Gita Rahasya

श्रेयो हि ज्ञानमभ्यासाज्ज्ञानाद् ध्यानं विशिष्यते ।
ध्यानात् कर्मफलत्यागस्त्यागाच्छान्तिनिरन्तरम् ॥ १२ ॥

(Better indeed is knowledge than scriptural study; better than knowledge is meditation; better than meditation is renunciation of the fruit of action; from renunciation results instantaneous peace – Bhagavad Gita Chapter 12 Verse 12)

In the context of geopolitical issues, the principle of Ahimsa encourages leaders and nations to seek peaceful resolutions to conflicts, prioritize dialogue over confrontation, and promote reconciliation rather than aggression. Applied geopolitically, the principle of Dharma calls for leaders and nations to act ethically and with integrity, respecting international laws and norms, and ensuring justice and fairness in their interactions with other countries and peoples. It reminds them that true leadership is not just about acquiring and wielding power but about using that power responsibly for the greater good and in alignment with universal principles of right conduct. This principle counters the ego-driven tendencies of power-hungry leaders, reminding them of the importance of empathy, compassion, and a genuine concern for the welfare of those they lead. In the context of humanitarian crises, Nishkama Karma encourages nations to provide aid and support to affected regions and populations without expecting anything in return, demonstrating solidarity and compassion. 'Vasudhaiva Kutumbakam' encourages nations to work together to address global challenges such as climate change, pandemics, and poverty. Vairagya teaches leaders and nations to pursue policies that prioritize long-term peace, stability, and sustainable development over short-term gains or power struggles. It encourages wise decision-making that considers the well-being of future generations and the planet as a whole. Spiritual wisdom and enlightenment can encourage approaching conflicts with wisdom, empathy, and a broader perspective that goes beyond national interests.

The "Gita Rahasya" teaches the importance of cultivating spiritual resilience and inner strength (atma-bal). This principle encourages leaders to maintain composure, clarity of vision, and equanimity in the face of adversity, uncertainty, and geopolitical pressures. It promotes a comprehensive approach to leadership that integrates spiritual values with pragmatic decision-making, fostering sustainable solutions to global challenges. Tilak emphasizes the concept of svadharma, or one's duty, as outlined in the Bhagavad Gita. Leaders are reminded of their responsibilities towards their people and the broader global community. Leaders are called upon to uphold principles of righteousness (dharma), fairness, and justice in their governance and international relations. Gita Rahasya offers a philosophical foundation that encourages leaders to transcend narrow interests and aspire towards a more just, compassionate, and harmonious world order.

Global Inequality

Global inequality remains one of the most pressing challenges, manifesting in stark disparities in income, wealth, life chances, access to resources, and opportunities across countries and across societies. At its core lies a profound imbalance where a minority enjoys immense prosperity while billions struggle with poverty, lack of basic necessities, and limited prospects for advancement. This inequality is perpetuated by systemic factors such as unequal distribution of resources, discriminatory policies, lack of access to education and healthcare, and barriers to economic mobility. The consequences are far-reaching, exacerbating social tensions, undermining social cohesion, and impeding sustainable development efforts worldwide. Despite growing awareness and advocacy, the persistence of global inequality is often compounded by widespread indifference among those who are more privileged or insulated from its immediate impacts. This indifference stems from a range of factors including ignorance of the extent and implications of inequality, perceptions of inevitability or the belief that it is beyond individual influence, and a focus on personal or national interests over global solidarity.

Both, Gita Rahasya, and Dnyaneshwari underscore the oneness of all beings and nations, advocating for co-operation and empathy across diverse socio-economic backgrounds. This calls for recognizing and addressing disparities with a sense of shared humanity and collective responsibility. They encourage individuals, communities, and nations to recognize their responsibilities in addressing systemic injustices and disparities. Provide equitable opportunities, social justice, and inclusive development policies that uplift marginalized populations and reduce socio-economic gaps. Tilak extends the concept of Dharma to societal and global contexts, advocating for fair and just treatment of all individuals regardless of their social status. This principle calls for policies and initiatives that promote equal access to education, healthcare, employment opportunities, and basic amenities, ensuring that every person can realize their full potential. Themes of selflessness and compassion emphasize the importance of empathy and solidarity in addressing global inequality. The authors urge societies to support initiatives that alleviate poverty, empower vulnerable communities, and promote social inclusion. Vairagya points towards cultivating a mindset of moderation, simplicity, and mindfulness in consumption patterns. This calls for redistributive policies and sustainable development practices that prioritize social welfare over profit maximization.

Fractured foundations – the erosion of the global moral fabric

Pure and naked selfishness or self-centredness never succeeds in the world; because, although physical and material pleasures may be desirable to everyone, yet, as is a matter of actual experience, if our happiness interferes with the happiness of others, those others will certainly do us harm

– Lokmanya Tilak in Gita Rahasya Ch. 4

Cause

In the ever-evolving world, the concept of a shared moral fabric seems increasingly fragile and fragmented. The term "moral fabric" refers to the collective values, principles, and ethical standards that bind societies and individuals together, providing a sense of cohesion and guiding behavior toward what is considered right or wrong. However, this fabric appears to be unravelling on a global scale, manifesting in various forms of ethical erosion and societal disarray. One of the primary factors contributing to the erosion of the global moral fabric is the pervasive influence of modernity and globalization. As societies become more integrated through technology, trade, and cultural exchange, traditional values and norms are often challenged or diluted. This phenomenon can be observed in the clash between traditional cultural practices and the spread of Western ideals of individualism and consumerism. For example, in many parts of the world, there is a growing tension between preserving Indigenous cultural values and adopting Western notions of progress and development, which can lead to confusion and moral ambiguity. Moreover, the rapid pace of technological advancement has introduced ethical dilemmas that were previously unimaginable. Issues such as data privacy, artificial intelligence, and genetic engineering pose significant challenges to our moral framework. For instance, the debate over the ethical implications of AI and its potential impact on employment, privacy, and human autonomy highlights the complexity of navigating moral decisions in a technologically driven world. Another critical factor contributing to the erosion of the global moral fabric is the rise of political polarization and ideological extremism. In many countries, political leaders and movements exploit divisions within societies, promoting narratives that prioritize power and ideology over ethical considerations and social cohesion. This polarization not only undermines trust in institutions but also erodes the moral foundations that underpin democratic governance and social justice. Furthermore, economic disparities and social inequality exacerbate the erosion of the moral fabric by perpetuating injustice and undermining solidarity within communities. The widening gap between the rich and the poor, both within and between countries, can lead to resentment, social unrest, and a breakdown of trust in societal institutions. This economic insecurity can also contribute to moral relativism, where individuals or groups prioritize their interests over broader ethical considerations.

In addition to these systemic factors, cultural shifts and changing social norms play a significant role in shaping the moral landscape. For example, evolving attitudes towards issues such as gender equality, LGBTQ+ rights, and environmental sustainability reflect changing societal values and norms. While these shifts can contribute to progress and social justice, they can also generate resistance and backlash from those who perceive these changes as threats to their traditional values and beliefs. Moreover, the erosion of the global moral fabric is compounded by the prevalence of misinformation and disinformation in the digital age. The spread of false or misleading information through social media and online platforms can distort public discourse, undermine trust in reliable sources of information, and contribute to a climate of uncertainty and moral confusion. This phenomenon not only challenges our ability to make informed ethical decisions but also fosters cynicism and apathy towards shared moral values.

Effect

Erosion in the global moral fabric reveals as a pervasive unravelling of ethical standards and values that underpin societies worldwide. This phenomenon permeates various aspects of human interaction, governance, and cultural norms, leading to profound effects that shape the collective conscience of humanity.

At its core, erosion in the global moral fabric diminishes trust and mutual respect among individuals and communities. When moral principles such as honesty, integrity, and compassion erode, social cohesion weakens, giving rise to heightened conflict and division. Trust, essential for meaningful human relationships and societal stability, becomes fragile when moral values are compromised. This erosion breeds skepticism and cynicism, corroding the very foundations upon which healthy societies are built. Moreover, the erosion of the moral fabric produces systemic injustices and inequalities. As ethical standards decay, exploitation and abuse flourish unchecked. Economic disparities widen as greed and self-interest override considerations of fairness and equity. Vulnerable populations suffer disproportionately, marginalized by systems that prioritize profit and power over human welfare. Injustices rooted in moral decay perpetuate cycles of poverty, discrimination, and disenfranchisement, further fracturing communities and hindering sustainable development. Erosion in the global moral fabric inevitably undermines governance and institutions. When leaders and decision-makers abandon ethical responsibilities, corruption and impunity proliferate. Public trust in authorities diminishes, leading to political instability and governance failures. Accountability mechanisms weaken as moral decay infiltrates legislative bodies, regulatory agencies, and law enforcement institutions. This erosion of moral integrity in governance erodes democratic principles, threatening the rule of law and undermining efforts to promote justice and equality. Culturally, the erosion of moral fabric leads to the commodification and trivialization of values once held sacred. Traditional virtues of empathy, altruism, and solidarity give way to a culture of materialism and instant gratification. Media and popular culture perpetuate superficial ideals, glorifying fame, and wealth at the expense of genuine human connection and spiritual fulfilment. As moral relativism spreads, ethical norms become increasingly subjective, making it challenging to foster a shared sense of right and wrong essential for a cohesive society. Furthermore, erosion in the global moral fabric contributes to environmental degradation and disregard for natural resources. As short-term gains outweigh long-term sustainability, ecosystems suffer from exploitation and neglect. The ethical imperative to preserve biodiversity and mitigate climate change is undermined by profit-driven decisions that prioritize immediate economic benefits over environmental stewardship. This short-sighted approach perpetuates environmental injustices, exacerbating ecological crises and threatening the well-being of future generations. Ultimately, the effects of erosion in the global moral fabric are interrelated and far-reaching, permeating every facet of human existence. They undermine the potential for collective progress and prosperity, perpetuating cycles of conflict, inequality, and environmental degradation.

Will it help to turn to Gita Rahasya and Dnyaneshwari?

The teachings found in the Dnyaneshwari and Gita Rahasya indeed offer deep insights into navigating the complexities of human morality and societal erosion in today's global context. These texts provide timeless wisdom that transcends their historical origins and speaks directly to the challenges we face in maintaining moral integrity and ethical conduct in our modern world.

Dnyaneshwari takes us to the essence of dharma and the paths to spiritual realization. Central to its teachings is the concept of selflessness and detachment from the fruits of one's actions, which is necessary in countering the erosion of moral values driven by selfish desires and greed. Dnyaneshwar emphasizes the idea of performing one's duties with dedication and surrendering the outcomes to a higher power, thereby fostering a mindset focused on service and duty rather than personal gain. This perspective can serve as a powerful antidote to the self-centeredness and moral relativism that contribute to the weakening of the global moral fabric. Tilak interprets the Gita's teachings in light of monism, stressing the importance of discerning the true nature of the self and understanding the interdependence of all beings. This holistic view promotes compassion, empathy, and a sense of responsibility towards others, fostering a sense of unity and harmony essential for addressing moral decay on a global scale. Tilak's insights into karma yoga underscore the significance of performing one's duties selflessly and with integrity, which can inspire individuals to uphold ethical standards in their personal and professional lives.

In today's networked world, where technological advancements and globalization have blurred traditional boundaries and values, the teachings of Dnyaneshwari and Gita Rahasya offer a timeless blueprint for restoring and strengthening the global moral fabric. By cultivating virtues such as humility, compassion, and honesty, individuals can contribute positively to their communities and societies, thereby creating ripple effects that extend far beyond individual actions. The emphasis on self-discipline and self-awareness found in these texts encourages individuals to introspect and align their thoughts, words, and deeds with higher principles of righteousness and universal harmony. The teachings of Dnyaneshwari and Gita Rahasya emphasize the importance of spiritual growth and inner transformation as foundational elements in addressing moral erosion. Sant Dnyaneshwar highlights the significance of knowledge, devotion, and disciplined action in attaining spiritual enlightenment and transcending ego-driven desires. This comprehensive approach not only fosters individual moral development but also cultivates a sense of oneness ness and mutual respect among diverse communities and cultures worldwide. Likewise, the Gita Rahasya provides a philosophical framework for understanding the deeper meanings of the Bhagavad Gita's teachings in relation to societal dynamics and ethical governance. Tilak's commentary interprets the Gita's relevance in guiding leaders and policymakers toward ethical decision-making and governance rooted in justice, compassion, and the welfare of all beings. By applying these principles in politics, economics, and social justice, the creation of a more just and harmonious global society can be achieved.

Both texts emphasize the importance of mindfulness and ethical conduct in interpersonal relationships and daily interactions. Sant Dnyaneshwar's teachings on dharma emphasize the significance of upholding moral values such as truthfulness, non-violence, and respect for others' rights and dignity. Similarly, Lokmanya Tilak's commentary reinforces the ethical principles of honesty, integrity, and accountability in all spheres of life, from personal relationships to professional responsibilities. As we navigate the complexities of the modern world, the wisdom of these texts can serve as a beacon of light, guiding us toward a future where moral integrity and ethical values are upheld and cherished by all.

Diverse challenges of the modern world

The enduring legacy of Gita Rahasya and Dnyaneshwari offers profound insights that can be applied to address several global problems. Here are some specific global issues where these teachings can nudge us in the right direction and influence our thinking and actions:

Environmental Degradation and Climate Change: Both texts emphasize the interdependence of all beings and the importance of living in harmony with nature. The concept of dharma in Dnyaneshwari includes the responsibility of humans towards the environment and future generations. By adopting principles of stewardship (karma yoga) and reducing desires (nishkama karma), individuals and societies can mitigate environmental degradation and climate change. Practices such as respecting natural resources, reducing consumption, and promoting sustainability align with these teachings.

Conflict and Violence: The teachings of non-violence (ahimsa) and compassion are central to both Gita Rahasya and Dnyaneshwari. Applying these principles can help in resolving conflicts peacefully at personal, community, and international levels. By fostering empathy, understanding, and dialogue, individuals and leaders can work toward reconciliation and conflict resolution, thus contributing to global peace and stability.

Ethical Governance and Corruption: Lokmanya Tilak's Gita Rahasya provides insights into ethical governance and leadership. The emphasis on duty (dharma) and integrity in public service can inspire policymakers and leaders to prioritize the welfare of all citizens' over personal gain. The concept of karma underscores the accountability of individuals for their actions and the inevitable consequences that result from unethical behavior such as corruption. Leaders and administrators are reminded that corrupt practices not only undermine societal trust and cohesion but also create negative karmic consequences that can perpetuate cycles of injustice and suffering. By cultivating awareness of karma, individuals in positions of power are encouraged to act with transparency, accountability, and ethical responsibility, thereby fostering a culture of integrity and trust in governance. The teachings of detachment (vairagya) and equanimity (samatvam) provide valuable insights into maintaining moral clarity and inner balance amidst the temptations and pressures of political power and material wealth. Leaders who cultivate inner detachment are less susceptible to the allure of corrupt practices and are better able to make decisions based on principles of justice and fairness rather than personal gain or vested interests. Equanimity allows leaders to navigate complex governance challenges with a calm and balanced mind, making informed decisions that prioritize the welfare of all stakeholders. In addition, the teachings of Gita Rahasya and Dnyaneshwari emphasize the importance of spiritual wisdom (jnana) and moral courage (dhairya) in confronting corruption and promoting good governance. Spiritual wisdom encourages leaders to cultivate a deep understanding of ethical principles and the oneness of all beings, guiding their decisions with compassion and foresight. Moral courage empowers leaders to confront corrupt practices and systemic injustices, even in the face of adversity or opposition, thereby setting a precedent for ethical leadership and accountability in governance.

Social Justice: Both texts advocate for social equality and the upliftment of marginalized communities. Dnyaneshwari discusses the concept of seva (selfless service) and the duty of individuals to contribute positively to society. In the context of social justice, adherence to dharma guides individuals, communities, and institutions in addressing systemic inequalities, discrimination, and marginalization by promoting policies and practices that ensure equitable opportunities and outcomes for all members of society. Leaders and individuals advocating for social justice are reminded that every action—whether positive or negative—affects the collective welfare and contributes to the creation of a just and equitable society. By cultivating awareness of karma, individuals are encouraged to act with compassion, empathy, and integrity in their interactions with others, thereby fostering a culture of mutual respect and understanding essential for social harmony and justice. Applied to the pursuit of social justice, nishkama karma encourages individuals and organizations to prioritize the well-being and rights of marginalized and vulnerable populations. Leaders and activists committed to social justice are motivated to advocate for policies and initiatives that address systemic barriers to equality and promote inclusive practices that uplift disadvantaged communities. Spiritual wisdom empowers individuals to challenge unjust structures and practices while promoting transformative change rooted in ethical principles and moral integrity. By integrating spiritual wisdom with practical actions for social justice, leaders and activists can contribute to dismantling barriers to equality and promoting sustainable solutions that empower marginalized communities and foster a more inclusive society.

Materialism and Consumerism: The teachings of detachment (vairagya) as discussed in these texts encourage individuals to cultivate a mindset of non-attachment to material possessions and external outcomes. Detachment does not imply renunciation of material life but rather a perspective that values inner peace and spiritual growth over the pursuit of transient material pleasures. Spiritual wisdom encourages individuals to seek inner transformation and self-awareness, recognizing that genuine happiness arises from within rather than from external possessions or achievements. The concept of karma reminds individuals that their actions—whether in acquiring wealth, consuming goods, or managing resources—have broader implications for society and the environment.

Educational Reform and Knowledge Dissemination: Both texts emphasize the importance of knowledge (jnana) and intellectual growth. Their teachings promote a student-centred approach to education that prioritizes the holistic development of learners, nurturing their intellectual curiosity, creativity, and moral integrity. Gita Rahasya encourages critical thinking and the pursuit of knowledge for societal benefit. The concept of holistic education as advocated in these scriptures emphasizes the importance of nurturing not only intellectual growth but also emotional, social, and spiritual development in students. Holistic education encourages educators to create learning environments that promote critical thinking, empathy, resilience, and people skills alongside academic achievement.

To summarize

In our exploration of contemporary reflections on the insights from Gita Rahasya and Dnyaneshwari, we are faced with a fundamental choice: whether to dismiss these teachings as mere rhetoric of a bygone era or to sincerely seek and embrace their enduring value. These scriptures, rooted in deep spiritual wisdom and ethical guidance, offer us timeless principles that resonate deeply with the complexities and challenges of our modern world. They invite us to reflect on the nature of our actions, the pursuit of true fulfilment beyond material wealth, and our union with all beings and the environment.

Choosing to heed these teachings means recognizing their relevance in navigating contemporary dilemmas—be it ethical governance, sustainable living, social justice, or geo-political conflicts. They challenge us to transcend superficial pursuits and cultivate a deeper understanding of ourselves and our place in the universe. By applying these insights, we can foster a society grounded in compassion, integrity, and holistic wisdom, where each individual's actions contribute to collective well-being and harmony. Conversely, dismissing these teachings risks overlooking valuable lessons that can guide us toward a more balanced and purposeful existence. It is in our willingness to engage with these insights, to reflect upon their implications for our lives and society, that we discover their transformative potential. Whether as individuals, communities, or global citizens, our choice to embrace the teachings from Gita Rahasya and Dnyaneshwari can lead us toward a path of greater awareness, empathy, and ethical responsibility.

At this crucial juncture, let us embrace the opportunity to explore, interpret, and apply these ancient teachings in ways that resonate with our contemporary realities. By doing so, we honour the wisdom of the past while charting a course toward a future where values of compassion, justice, and spiritual growth serve as guiding ideals in a world faced with ever-evolving challenges and opportunities for positive change.

Chapter 11

Parting Thoughts

Final reflections

God unites, Religion divides

The title 'God unites, Religion divides' captures a serious dichotomy about the dual nature of human spirituality and collective identity. It exposes the complex interplay between spiritual unity and religious fragmentation. At its core, this notion suggests that while the idea of a divine or superior entity often serves as a unifying force among believers, organized religions—through their doctrines, rituals, and institutional structures, have historically been sources of division and conflict among human societies.

God, in various religious traditions, represents the ultimate source of unity and transcendence. Believers perceive God as the creator of the universe, the embodiment of absolute truth, or the ultimate reality that transcends individual and collective human experiences. The belief in a higher power often fosters a sense of oneness and shared purpose among adherents, regardless of cultural or geographical differences. Across different faith traditions, the notion of a divine presence or sacred force serves as a unifying principle that provides solace, guidance, and a moral compass for navigating life's challenges. However, the unity inherent in the concept of God contrasts sharply with the divisive nature of organized religions. Religion, as a human construct, encompasses complex systems of beliefs, practices, rituals, and institutional frameworks that shape collective identity and social norms within specific communities. While these structures can provide cohesion, moral guidance, and a sense of belonging to their adherents, they also have the potential to create divisions based on doctrinal differences, interpretations of sacred texts, and competing claims to religious authority. Historically, conflicts and tensions rooted in religious differences have led to ideological disputes, sectarian violence, and even wars. Throughout centuries, religious divisions have been evident in the clashes between different religious groups, the persecution of religious minorities, and the imposition of religious orthodoxy through state power. These divisions often stem from human interpretations and applications of religious teachings, which can vary widely across time and geographical contexts. Moreover, the institutionalization of religion—through organized churches, mosques, temples, synagogues, and religious hierarchies— can sometimes prioritize institutional survival, doctrinal purity, and political influence over the spiritual principles of compassion, tolerance, and unity espoused by religious founders and scriptures. This divergence between religious ideals and institutional practices has contributed to perceptions of hypocrisy, intolerance, and exclusivity within and between religious communities.

In contemporary society, the tension between the unifying potential of belief in God and the divisive reality of organized religion remains palpable. Globalization, migration, and digital connectivity have brought diverse religious traditions into closer proximity, fostering both dialogue and discord among believers of different faiths. At the same time, secularism and the rise of non-religious identities have challenged the privileged status of organized religions in shaping public discourse and policymaking.

I believe this invites reflection on the complex interplay between spirituality, organized religion, and human identity. It recognizes the profound role of belief in a higher power as a source of unity and moral guidance, while also acknowledging the historical and contemporary challenges posed by religious divisions and institutional complexities. There is clearly a need to realise the potential for interfaith dialogue and cooperation to bridge divides and foster greater understanding in the increasingly interconnected modern-day world. Finally, delineating God and religion will serve to clarify concepts, promote respectful dialogue, encourage personal exploration of spirituality, facilitate critical analysis, and uphold principles of religious freedom and diversity in pluralistic societies.

Essence of transcendental literature

Transcendental or timeless literature by its nature is not static and most certainly creates (and leaves) space to accommodate newer interpretations, insights, and wisdom. Such works of literature act as living dialogues, shaped and enriched by the experiences and wisdom of those who study them. A timeless literature transcends time, with each generation reinterpreting and expanding upon the foundational ideas.

One striking feature of transcendental literature like the Bhagavad Gita is its open-endedness. It does not present rigid dogmas; instead, it offers frameworks of wisdom that can evolve as human understanding and experience expand. This accumulation of knowledge over centuries mirrors a kind of philosophical evolution, where the core essence of the work remains, but its meanings are shaped by the intellectual, cultural, and spiritual ambience of different eras.

Accretion to a seminal work such as Bhagavad Gita, happens not just through scholars and sages but also through everyday readers who approach these texts with new questions and new experiences. Each new generation that interacts with the Gita (or similar works like the Tao Te Ching) adds a layer of interpretation that keeps it vibrant and ever relevant. In a way, such transcendental works of literature mirror the essence of the universe itself – dynamic, ever-changing, yet grounded in timeless principles.

Bhagavad Gita is not just a religious text

The dual perception of the Mahabharata and Bhagavad Gita is somewhat ironical. The Mahabharata itself is traditionally viewed as an epic narrative, rich with stories, legends, and chronicles of dynastic struggles embedded within its sprawling narrative. Despite being a part of the Mahabharata, the Gita however, is often segregated and revered as a distinct religious text.

The Mahabharata, as one of the longest epic poems in the world, enjoys widespread accessibility and appreciation as a layered narrative fabric that weaves together heroic tales, moral dilemmas, and philosophical insights within the context of ancient Indian society. Its expansive scope and diverse characters resonate with readers as a reflection of human complexities and societal dynamics across cultures and epochs. The epic's portrayal of familial conflict, ethical quandaries, and the pursuit of justice on the battlefield of Kurukshetra provides a timeless backdrop for exploring themes that transcend temporal and cultural boundaries. In contrast, the Bhagavad Gita, though a pivotal section of the Mahabharata, is often approached primarily through a lens of religious reverence and spiritual guidance. This perception of the Bhagavad Gita as primarily a religious text can create a sense of distance for some readers who view it through the lens of specific religious doctrines or rituals. Categorization of literature as religious can create a perception of being complex, elite, and inaccessible to a common reader. Moreover, it may be perceived as exclusive to followers of that particular faith or belief system, potentially alienating those who do not identify with or practice the religion in question. This perspective can overshadow Gita's broader significance as a philosophical and ethical guide that offers universal wisdom applicable to all individuals seeking clarity on moral dilemmas, the nature of existence, and the pursuit of spiritual enlightenment.

The Bhagavad Gita actually transcends the confines of religion to offer profound philosophical and spiritual teachings that are universally applicable. One of the key reasons why the Bhagavad Gita should not be narrowly categorized as a religious text lies in its universal appeal and relevance beyond any specific faith or tradition. While it emerged within the context of ancient Indian culture and philosophy, its teachings are not bound by sectarian beliefs or rituals. Instead, the Gita offers timeless wisdom that addresses fundamental human concerns and dilemmas, such as ethical decision-making, the pursuit of spiritual growth, and the attainment of inner peace amidst external challenges. The Gita's teachings on karma (action) and dharma (duty/righteousness) underscore the importance of ethical conduct and responsibility, guiding individuals to act in accordance with their inherent nature and societal roles while maintaining a sense of detachment from personal desires and outcomes. This universal ethical framework applies to people of all backgrounds and beliefs, offering practical guidance on how to live a meaningful and purposeful life while adhering to moral principles. Furthermore, the Bhagavad Gita presents a holistic view of spirituality that encompasses the unity of all beings and the unity of life. It emphasizes the concept of the self (atman) as immortal and beyond the physical body, highlighting the unity of all living beings and their underlying unity with the divine (Brahman). This non-dualistic perspective challenges rigid religious boundaries and invites individuals to transcend limited identities and recognize the underlying unity of existence. Moreover, the Gita's teachings on devotion (bhakti) emphasize the importance of cultivating a loving relationship with the divine through heartfelt devotion and surrender. This path of devotion is not exclusive to any particular religious tradition but is accessible to anyone seeking a deeper connection with the spiritual dimension of life. The Gita's emphasis on love, compassion, and selflessness as essential qualities for spiritual growth resonates across cultures and beliefs, encouraging individuals to cultivate virtues that foster harmony and unity within themselves and with others. Another significant aspect of the Bhagavad Gita that distinguishes it from a religious scripture is its emphasis on self-inquiry and the pursuit of knowledge (jnana). The Gita encourages individuals to question the nature of reality, the purpose of life, and the true identity of the self. Through introspection and contemplation, seekers are invited to transcend superficial identities and attachments, gaining insight into the eternal essence that underlies all existence.

Recognizing the Gita's universal appeal and relevance can help appreciate its teachings as a source of inspiration and practical wisdom that enriches the lives of people from diverse cultural, religious, and philosophical backgrounds.

Fading Echoes – the erosion of historical awareness in the post-modern age

In this postmodern era, characterized by rapid technological advancements, cultural shifts, and evolving social norms, there is a discernible trend of distancing ourselves from history and losing touch with ancient texts that have shaped civilizations for centuries. This phenomenon raises critical questions about our relationship with the past, the value of historical knowledge, and the implications of such distancing on our collective understanding and identity.

As we slip deeper into the postmodern era, there is a noticeable shift towards a focus on the present and the future, often at the expense of historical awareness. Postmodernism, with its emphasis on relativism, skepticism towards grand narratives, and celebration of plurality, tends to prioritize the immediacy of experiences and narratives that are current or easily relatable. This can lead to a diminished interest in exploring the complexities and lessons embedded in ancient texts that offer insights into human thought, morality, and societal structures of bygone eras. Moreover, the relentless pace of technological innovation and digitalization in the postmodern age has contributed to a shrinking attention span and a preference for information that is instantly accessible and consumable. Ancient texts, often dense and requiring deep engagement, may struggle to compete with the immediacy and convenience offered by modern forms of media and communication. This shift poses a challenge to the preservation and dissemination of historical knowledge, as ancient texts risk becoming relegated to specialized academic circles rather than being widely accessible and understood by the broader public.

As societies globalize and cultures intermingle in the postmodern world, there is a tendency to prioritize contemporary issues and universal values over the specificities and complexities of local histories and ancient texts. This can lead to a homogenization of cultural identities and a loss of appreciation for the rich embroidery of narratives that have shaped diverse civilizations over millennia. Ancient texts, with their unique cultural perspectives and ethical frameworks, offer invaluable insights into the human condition and provide a foundation for understanding the roots of contemporary beliefs and practices. Literature's role as a carrier of generational wisdom should be acknowledged. The implications of distancing ourselves from history and ancient texts are deep. By neglecting these foundational texts, we risk losing touch with the wisdom, traditions, and cultural heritage that have shaped our societies. Ancient texts not only provide historical context but also offer timeless teachings that remain relevant across generations. They serve as a bridge between the past and the present, offering perspectives that challenge our assumptions and encourage critical reflection on contemporary issues.

Revive and Rediscover

Periodic revival of ancient texts fosters spiritual renewal and ethical introspection. In the turbulent landscape of the modern world, where technological advancements vie with societal upheavals and individual crises of identity, there exists a serious need for reviving and reviewing ancient texts such as the Bhagavad Gita, the Bible, or the Quran. The rediscovery of rich ancient texts through credible and genuine commentaries will reconnect individuals with their cultural heritage, grounding them in traditions that emphasize universal principles. Such revivals will offer holistic frameworks for personal growth and ethical decision-making, promoting inner harmony and resilience amidst external turmoil. Moreover, the rediscovery of ancient texts is essential to foster intergenerational dialogue and continuity of wisdom. As societies evolve and face new challenges, the insights gleaned from texts like the Bhagavad Gita and its commentaries provide a touchstone for evaluating contemporary issues through a lens of ethical integrity and spiritual depth.

Medium of rediscovery

Rediscovery of ancient literature at periodic intervals to calibrate the narrative to suit contemporary needs can occur through various mediums, each offering unique advantages in engaging with and interpreting these rich texts.

Written Texts - This includes translation, adaptations, and interpretations of ancient texts. Written texts preserve the original language and structure of the literature, allowing for meticulous study of the nuances, symbolism, and cultural context embedded within the works. Writers and readers analyze written texts to unravel layers of meaning and explore the philosophical, moral, and narrative dimensions of ancient literature.

Commentaries and Annotations - Commentaries provide critical analysis and interpretation of ancient texts. These annotations often accompany translations or stand-alone editions, offering insights into historical context, linguistic nuances, and philosophical interpretations. Annotations serve as guides for readers, helping to navigate complex ideas and themes within ancient literature.

Scholarly Studies and Research Papers - Academic research and scholarly studies contribute to the rediscovery of ancient literature by exploring themes, trends, and influences across different texts and cultures. Scholars publish research papers, articles, and books that dive deep into specific aspects of ancient literature, such as literary techniques, philosophical concepts, and socio-cultural contexts.

Digital Archives and Online Resources - Digital platforms and online repositories make ancient texts more accessible to a global audience. Libraries, museums, and academic institutions digitize manuscripts and ancient documents, making them available for online study and research. Digital archives also provide tools for textual analysis, comparison of different versions, and collaborative research efforts.

Public Lectures and Discourses: Scholars, educators, and experts deliver public lectures, seminars, and workshops on ancient literature. These discourses provide opportunities for interactive engagement with texts through spoken word, interpretation, and discussion. Public lectures often explore the relevance of ancient wisdom to contemporary issues, fostering dialogue and critical reflection among participants.

Performances and Dramatic Interpretations - Some ancient texts, particularly epics and dramatic works, are rediscovered through performances and dramatic interpretations. Theatre productions, staged readings, and adaptations bring ancient stories to life, offering audiences a visceral and emotive experience of the narratives, characters, and moral dilemmas presented in the literature.

Artistic and Creative Expressions - Visual artists, musicians, filmmakers, and other creative professionals draw inspiration from ancient literature to create artworks, compositions, films, and multimedia projects. These artistic expressions reinterpret ancient themes, motifs, and narratives through contemporary lenses, fostering cross-cultural dialogue and appreciation for the enduring relevance of ancient texts.

Educational Programs and Courses - Academic institutions offer courses, workshops, and educational programs focused on ancient literature. These programs introduce students to foundational texts, guide them through close reading and analysis, and encourage critical thinking about the cultural, historical, and philosophical dimensions of ancient literature.

Through these diverse mediums, ancient literature continues to be rediscovered, interpreted, and appreciated across diverse cultures and generations. Each medium contributes uniquely to the preservation, dissemination, and exploration of the timeless wisdom and artistic achievements found within ancient texts.

Finally, I urge readers to realise the value locked in ancient literature. Dnyaneshwar and Tilak, separated by centuries yet united in their reverence for spiritual wisdom, have left us enduring legacies that transcend cultural boundaries and speak to the universal quest for truth and enlightenment. As a final word, I pay homage to these visionary authors in Vedavyasa, Sant Dnyaneshwar and Lokmanya Tilak, whose works continue to inspire and guide us, encouraging a renewed appreciation for ancient texts and their enduring relevance.

Methodology adopted for the comparative and contemporary analysis

This comparative and contemporary analysis of "Gita Rahasya" by Bal Gangadhar Tilak and "Dnyaneshwari" by Sant Dnyaneshwar employed a structured methodology to explore their respective interpretations of the Bhagavad Gita.

Strengths of this approach include its systematic comparison of themes, philosophical perspectives, and socio-cultural contexts presented in both texts. It also involved referring to various commentaries and insights offered by multiple thinkers and scholars. By juxtaposing Tilak's socio-political analysis in "Gita Rahasya" with Dnyaneshwar's devotional and philosophical commentary in "Dnyaneshwari," the analysis highlights diverse interpretations and applications of the Gita's teachings across different epochs. However, this methodology also has limitations. It relies heavily on subjective interpretations of the texts, influenced by the authors' historical contexts and personal ideologies. Variations in translation and interpretation may lead to discrepancies in understanding subtle nuances of the original Marathi/Sanskrit verses. Moreover, the comparative analysis may oversimplify complex philosophical ideas and overlook the deeper spiritual dimensions embedded within the texts. Despite these challenges, the comparative and contemporary analysis of "Gita Rahasya" and "Dnyaneshwari" endeavours to offer insights into how ancient scriptures continue to inform and inspire diverse interpretations in our modern world.

The author does not claim authority or scholarly expertise over the Bhagavad Gita, Gita Rahasya, or Dnyaneshwari. This enterprise was born out of a curious mind to explore how literature evolves as it transitions between generations while accumulating added wisdom and gaining more relevance. I found the Bhagavad Gita as a unique medium to study this evolution of literature for several reasons. Gita is a highly revered text, is globally accepted, has been interpreted at periodic intervals and through generations through authentic inquiry by credible luminaries, and finally my familiarity with these two texts and the language medium.

References

(other than cited under the respective chapters)

Sant Dnyaneshwar (1290 CE) - Dnyaneshwari

Bal Gangadhar Tilak (1915) - Srimad Bhagavad Gita Rahasya athwa Karmayogashastra (Marathi)

M R Yardi (1991) – Shri Jnanadeva's Bhavarth Dipika

Ranade R.D (1995) – Sant Dnyaneshwar: Life and Works

B R Sukhtankar (1934) – English translation of Tilak's Gita Rahasya

Kulkarni G A (1982) – Dnyaneshwari: A philosophical analysis

Pradhan V G (1948) – Dnyaneshwari translation in English

https://archive.org/details/tilak-gita-rahasya-english_202010/page/n3/mode/2up

https://archive.org/details/Srimad_bhagavad_gita_rahasya-marathi-bal_gangadhar_tilak_1924/page/n41/mode/2up

https://www.santsahitya.in/dnyaneshwari-in-marathi

Wikipedia

Other Articles, Essays, e-books, and other resources from the internet reached through Google Search that discuss themes related to "Dnyaneshwari," "Gita Rahasya," and their comparative analysis.

While every effort has been made to thoroughly cite all sources used in authoring this book, some materials and references may have been inadvertently omitted. The intent has been to provide a comprehensive and accurate account of the research, but due to the extensive nature of the sources consulted, certain references might not be explicitly noted. The author regrets any oversights and acknowledges that the omission of these references does not diminish the contribution of the cited works to the research. Any errors or omissions are unintentional, and feedback or corrections regarding references are welcomed to ensure the integrity and completeness of future revisions.

Reader Notes